Building Positive Parent and School Partnerships

Building Positive Parent and School Partnerships

Using Alternative Dispute Resolution Communication Skills and Strategies

Marc Purchin

Published by Purchin Consulting Inc.
Culver City, California
www.purchinconsulting.com

Building Positive Parent and School Partnerships: Using Alternative Dispute Resolution Communication Skills and Strategies

First published 2023

ISBN: 979-8-9887151-2-2

Contents

Preface

When I was practically an infant, specialists at UCLA told my parents I had severe learning disabilities and that I needed a lot of support. The doctors went on to say I had very little chance of earning a high school diploma. Obviously I wasn't aware of these conversations, but this is how my parents interpreted them and, as I got older, the conversations were recounted to me from their point of view.

I will tell you that from around age three, I knew there was something "wrong" with me. I didn't speak until I was about that age. I remember going to see a speech therapist once or twice a week. I also went to a clinic to work on motor skills like balance. This speech and motor clinic – today likely called an occupational therapy clinic – was located forty-five minutes to an hour from where I lived. Going three times a week for five years was a lot to endure – not only for me but for my parents.

So I know from personal experience just how complicated, frustrating, and demoralizing it can be to navigate the educational system from the perspective of a student with special needs. I have devoted my professional career to helping parents and educators of such students, with most of my success centered on the methods of Alternative Dispute Resolution (ADR).

ADR provides an opportunity for individuals to resolve disagreements in a safe, efficient way. The process is voluntary and confidential, such that everyone involved must be willing participants who are open to finding common ground; to be problem-solving partners instead of adversaries. The intention is to move through conflict in the fastest and easiest way possible, thereby reducing tensions – and legal costs – for both parents and school districts.

No wonder federal and state education departments have provided grant money as incentives for school districts to use ADR to resolve disputes at an early stage without the need to go to due process. This workbook provides ADR skills and techniques that *both* parents and district employees can use. It doesn't take sides because it is based on the premise that we're all on the same side, namely to resolve issues to the satisfaction of all those concerned – so that students can thrive.

It's a professional mission with added personal meaning because of my own related background. As such, it has been a privilege to write *Building Positive Parent and School Partnerships*. And I gratefully dedicate it to all the educators who have chosen to work with students and families that have learning challenges. I also dedicate this book to all the wonderful parents who are naturally committed to advocating for their child, while also maintaining a positive relationship with their child's school.

Now well into my third decade in this business, I've never met any educator who chose to get their degrees and credentials because they wanted to make the lives of their colleagues and families a waking nightmare. And I never met any parent who had a child with a disability because they wanted to make the lives of the school and the district miserable.

This is hard and personal work. For many of you, you've chosen this field for personal reasons. I understand that very well, and I hope you will see this book as a friendly and useful tool to help navigate through some challenging times.

To my parents and many of the educators I had growing up: Thank you for your advocacy and not giving up on me. These people include Betty McCloud, the speech therapist who taught me how to talk and how to be understood, and Gary Codon, my resource teacher in high school who stood up for me when some of my teachers didn't understand my disability. One example I remember vividly is when my health teacher gave me a D grade because he saw me in a play excelling and

knowing all my lines. (I wasn't able to memorize some of the key concepts for his exam.) So he snarled at me, "You are just lazy or goofing off.
You can memorize lines in a play but you can't pass a test in health class?"
Mr. Codon was an able advocate who explained to the health teacher
that my brain works very well – just differently – and persuaded him I
wasn't simply goofing off.

I feel so lucky to have gotten through it all, with help, and found
my way into a career I enjoy; one that allows me to wake up every morn-
ing and partner with school and parent teams that may be struggling and
at the same time sincerely want to work their way through the hard stuff
in order to focus back on the student.

Acknowledgments

My gratitude has fewer limitations than my memory, so forgive me if you are one of those colleagues and friends I neglected to mention here, but who nonetheless contributed to the development of this book. After all, everyone agrees there's no "I" in "team."

Well, there's also no "I" in "We are so much better when we collaborate, and lucky when our partners are also our pals." So, for all the help and support, my deepest thanks go to these good folks:

Editor and rewriter: Richard Scaffidi
Podcast collaborators: Erica Marx, Gail Nugent, Fran Goldfarb,
   Anthony Farenga, Jaime Tate-Symons; and producer Kevin Higa

Introduction

This is a workbook for both educators and parents. I've spent nearly thirty years helping build positive parent and school partnerships, especially when it comes to Individualized Education Program (IEP) teams. Now I want to share many of the top tips, tools, and skills that I have found helpful for establishing positive communication and building healthy productive relationships – especially between parents and schools.

I know that most of you are very busy, so I have taken the best tips and skills and then distilled them into concise chapters that each describe a central idea and its corresponding skill. Each chapter and skill includes easily relatable examples and offers practical suggestions of ways you can deepen your understanding of these ideas and techniques, then sharpen them with real-world exercises you can practice on your own and with those around you.

I'm always eager to hear about what does or doesn't work for you from these chapters and ways to practice the skills. If a chapter leaves you with questions or suggestions, I would love to hear what you have to say. Maybe you've had success with practicing an exercise, or even better, had a win using some of these skills in a real life situation. Are there other tips and insights that could help your colleagues or fellow parents? Email me at mpurchin@purchinconsulting.com and I will post your good ideas on my website for everyone to see. After all, we are truly in this together, breathing the same air and sharing the same road.

For added benefit, use this book in combination with the related podcasts as well as direct access to monthly virtual office hours. It's a **three-part approach:**

1. The **book** is not meant to stand alone, nor is it meant to get dusty on the shelf, so keep it handy and refer to it often, as each chapter illuminates a proven communication skill, including suggested ways to practice with trusted colleagues or friends.
2. The **podcasts** are my informal recorded interviews and conversations with top professionals who use these exact skills on a daily basis.
3. The **virtual office hours** are here for you so that you may feel free to "drop by" monthly to share or inquire about anything related to the book and how it may apply to situations in your own experience. It is also a safe place to practice or workshop the tools and exercises mentioned in this book. Plus it's a golden opportunity to learn from each other.

Naturally I gave thought to the order of the chapters in the book, and that order makes sense to me, with my firm recommendation that everyone needs to start by reading "It's All About Active Listening" (page 1), as it is foundational for integrating the rest of the chapters and skills.

Yet I also intentionally wrote this book so that the chapters can be read in any order. My hope is that whether you have several hours or only a few minutes, you can pick up this user-friendly workbook and find a skill or topic that interests you, or that may apply to a situation you'd like to prepare for. My deeper hope is that you will gradually integrate these concepts and tools into your everyday interactions, as this really is a practical manual for handling challenging conversations in a positive manner during just about any dispute.

Still, the main goal is for parents and school teams to be on the same page (almost literally), to be able to work through differences using consistent, clear, proven techniques that make problem-solving a cooperative, respectful, even friendly process – all driven by the shared motivation to best serve a student's needs. There's little need for *outside* mediators when people *in* the meeting have mediator skills.

It's All About
Active Listening

This is the first chapter for a reason: Each chapter after this one is essentially a facet of active listening.

Variations of this "umbrella" skill are offered throughout this book, in chapters such as "The Art of the Question," "Don't Argue Mentally," "Separating Interests from Positions," and "Saying a Lot Without Saying a Thing." As you review each of them, you'll recognize their similarities as well as their differences, and you'll begin to distinguish which tools and skills best fit a given situation – but their common thread is active listening.

So let's start with the definition. Am I allowed to quote Wikipedia? Okay, don't judge:

> Active listening is the practice of preparing to listen, observing what verbal and nonverbal messages are being sent, and then providing appropriate feedback for the sake of showing attentiveness to the message being presented. Active listening is listening on purpose.

If we were to survey communication experts – and since I'm an occasional betting man – I'd wager that an overwhelming majority would say that active listening is the most important skill. So when I train people to be neutral meeting facilitators and mediators, it is the first lesson. It is a communication skill in which the mediator recognizes and validates the emotional context of the person who is speaking. It builds trust between mediator and speaker, demonstrates understanding and acceptance, and encourages discussion of important issues.

Speaking of important issues, what causes you to get mad? Did you get mad because you didn't get something specific? Or is that you didn't feel heard? Yep, that last answer is the correct one more often than not.

Listening builds trust, demonstrates understanding and acceptance, and encourages discussion.

It is always better to seek to understand than to seek to be understood. That may sound like it came out of a fortune cookie, but think about it: You can make a brilliant proposal, but you'll never convince the person who didn't listen. Don't be that one yourself and maybe miss out on a brilliant proposal. In fact, strive to be such a good listener that you'll respectfully hear every proposal, because you just might come across brilliance where you least expect it.

Here's an example. Imagine I am a school principal. It's a busy day and I have a lot on my plate. A parent comes to see me about a concern with her child's teacher. Her position is that the child must be placed in a different (supposedly better) teacher's class. She appears pretty angry – and since I have an open-door policy – I ought to take this opportunity to use my active listening skills to begin getting at the underlying interests of this parent.

I decide that since the parent's emotions are running hot (and it's not the best time for me) I am going to pause on giving *my* position, which might include a desire to defend the current teacher. But that would be a bad move at this time, probably escalating the conversation to a butting-heads conflict.

Instead of that, I will say, "Thank you for coming in today and letting me know about your concern. I want to give you a thoughtful response, so how about I take the next twenty-four hours to do some thinking, and perhaps some consultation. Meanwhile, before we leave our conversation today, help me understand what led you to this request. I want to have all the information and be sure I fully understand your interests."

That gently measured approach accomplishes several good things. No hasty decisions are made. No stubborn stances are dug in deeper. Everybody's interests are being respectfully considered. A concerned parent feels heard and validated by a responsible principal who has set the tone for a productive partnership. A serious path forward is articulated. In short, a potential confrontation is now a promising collaboration.

One thing about active listening that I particularly like is that nobody has to have all the answers. Naturally when someone comes to us with a problem, we want to fix it. But active listening comes first; fixing, and even just giving suggestions, comes after. In between we must make sure that we are talking with people in a way that lets them know they are being heard. You can show it with eye contact, leaning into the conversation, asking clarifying questions, and so on.

Yes, we're in these meetings seeking agreement, and it may take a while to reach a final resolution, but the more time we take in an early stage, the less time we are going to spend in a formal mediation or litigation. So if that means pausing to collect our thoughts, to clarify interests, and to lower the emotional temperature, so be it. That amounts not to time lost, but to time well spent; time to build a more open, trusting team that cares enough to *listen*.

Practicing This Skill

Partner up for a role-playing exercise! Partner A takes one uninterrupted minute to rant about anything, perhaps including a demand. Partner B *actively listens* until the minute expires, then responds to Partner A, keeping in mind that Partner B is not able to agree or solve Partner A's problem in any way (at least not on the spot). Partner B's job is to simply acknowledge and make sure that Partner A is heard.

Then swap roles, or for larger groups, rotate participants,

each using a different rant, of course. Debrief and assess what worked well or not, and why.

For bonus points, did Partner A indirectly reveal underlying emotions or agendas that might be useful in later getting to a truer resolution? If so, then we're well on our way to the other chapters and skills, such as "Separating Interests from Positions" (page 22).

Continue on to the remaining chapters in this book. My hope is that each time you read one – and get to practice using a skill or tool in it – the lightbulb in your head will go on and you'll say to yourself, "Oh, yeah…I get it, and I want to use it!"

The Art of the Question

If you want to have a successful parent-school meeting, or any important conversation, really, then come prepared with a well-stocked kit of useful questions as well as positive techniques for asking them. This skill set is hugely valuable, and crafting it requires more art than science.

It may be a formal IEP meeting, a parent-teacher conference, a phone call with a service provider such as a speech therapist or behaviorist, or a school staff meeting; you name it. In each such situation, the right questions and other conversation starters can advance the dialogue in safe and helpful ways because they are specifically phrased to encourage participation by all, and they model a tone of mutual respect. Beginning with an artful question, you can establish an atmosphere most likely to gain productive and collaborative outcomes.

The relationship between parent and school needs to be a partnership, not a competition. If a meeting actively emphasizes finding common ground rather than taking sides, everyone there can be a winner. Besides, aren't we all on the student's side? Sure, there will be participants who arrive stressed, angry, or itching for conflict. But it only makes matters worse if the conversation begins with words that feel like challenges.

Let's call them Questionable Questions. They include pretty much any yes-or-no question and most "why" questions. Bad attitudes and arguments are provoked by questions such as, "Do you have a problem with our decision?" or "Why are you so upset?" or "Is it right for teachers to treat students like this?" or "Why won't your child behave?"

When someone comes at us with a predetermined position or demand (see "Separating Interests from Positions," page 22), we want to keep things as friendly and neutral as possible. That's why open-ended questions are best, as they bring responses that help us understand more about the issue at hand and – equally important – avoid defensiveness.

Asking questions can assist others to resolve their own problems.

Here is an example. A parent declares, "I want a one-to-one aide for my son." A responder's instinct may be to react defensively, such as saying, "In order for a student to qualify for an aide, we have to do an assessment." Or, "There is already a three-to-one ratio of students to adults in the class." We may very well get to those points later, but let's start off with a gentler response, such as, "Can you tell me more about your concerns? How might an aide be helpful?"

By phrasing the question that way, with sincere curiosity and open-ness, the parent's answer can't just be to dig in and repeat the demand. Instead, it might very well reveal underlying interests or concerns that could open the door to discussing that request – among other alternatives. For instance, maybe the child has expressed feelings of being unsafe, or poses a risk for running away if left briefly unsupervised. Those are understandable anxieties, and worthy of addressing, but employing a one-to-one aide may not be the solution at all, with other steps and measures more reasonable and available.

Moving on: Of course an unasked question is usually trouble. We have all been in that conversation where we had no clue what the person was talking about; sometimes leaving the conversation more confused than when we entered. Here's a recent example in a special education context.

A parent I'd been working with was told by a district representative that it is the district's responsibility to provide "fape." This acronym, FAPE, stands for "free and appropriate public education," but the parent didn't know that, and was embarrassed to admit it. So she waited until after the meeting to call me. I told her she wasn't alone in her confusion, that we in the profession use way too many abbreviations and insider lingo. I also assured her that we want her to ask clarifying questions, that it's an essential – and welcome – part of the IEP team meeting process. (And shame on me for assuming everybody knows that IEP stands for Individualized Education Program!)

Parents and district staff should ask helpful questions to ensure not only that we understand what is being said, but also to clarify understanding the interests of the person who is speaking. Likewise, it is a responsibility of speakers to make sure they are being understood.

So, in the illustration above, a learning point for the district representative was the need to frequently check in with the parent, to be certain they were on the same page throughout the conversation. Employing effective question strategies would have easily prevented the problem, as would using skills for spotting nonverbal signals, such as a listener's facial expressions that suggest confusion or suspicion. (See page 59 for "Saying a Lot Without Saying a Thing.")

Asking questions – the right ones, that is – can also be useful when assisting others to resolve their own problems. People will come to me for advice, often even wanting me to tell them the solution. Instead, by posing a few artful questions, I'm likely to uncover just what the true interests are. This helps frame the issues so that they may effectively problem-solve for themselves. And when they do, they feel much more ownership than if I overtly advise them or give them direction.

Key Takeaways from This Skill

1. Ask when you simply don't understand.
2. Ask in order to clarify underlying interests.
3. Ask only helpful questions that advance focus and productivity. These should be neutral, nonconfrontational, and open-ended.
4. Don't ask yes-or-no or "why" questions.

Practicing This Skill

A great way to become an effective questioner is to continually ask yourself – prior to and perhaps even during these meetings – what you hope to accomplish. Specifically: What truths can you find in what the other person is saying? What exactly did you hear them say? Does understanding this better help you understand their perspective? How so? How can what you are hearing today open new possibilities for a resolution? How did you come to this idea, belief, or value of a resolution?

Below are ten suggested conversation starters and questions. Review them, and come up with others on your own. Then consider carrying them around in your wallet! When you are in a meeting or conversation, practice the art of questioning by trying them out.

- Tell me more about...
- I'm not sure I understand the part about...
- Help me understand.
- What would you like to see happen today?
- Let me summarize what you just said.
- I gather you have been discouraged about...
- It would help me if I understood better how you came to decide on this specific request.
- What would it look like to you if this were resolved/not resolved?
- What will the program look like without this part?
- I want to thank you for discussing such a hard issue with us, and hope you can tell us more about...

Set Team Agreements

L ike it or not, we are going to encounter conflict. One of the first goals at my training sessions is for attendees to understand and accept that reality. Next, however, I move on to a sure method of limiting conflict, namely establishing ground rules for meetings – although I prefer the term *agreements* because it better conveys collaboration and positivity. It's – you know – more "agreeable."

Over the years I've learned the importance of setting healthy procedural and behavioral guidelines and boundaries so that we can efficiently and safely work through whatever conflicts arise. It's why a successful meeting begins with agreement on the way we are going to communicate.

By studying workplace tensions, specifically at school sites, I know that working through conflict allows an opportunity for growth and improved relationships. We've all suffered through meetings where there have been disparate perspectives, contradictory opinions, and even entirely different agendas. Consider an Individualized Education Program (IEP) team meeting. To be productive, it requires all participants to agree on several issues: a specified agenda; an atmosphere of respect and clear communication; and that each member will strive to listen and understand. Most of all, everyone must stay focused on the needs of the student being discussed.

At the start of each and every IEP meeting (this works for all kinds of meetings), the facilitator should take a moment to get agreement on basic procedures and norms. Ideally, that includes asking participants if there are any agreements that should be added. Even if you are not the person running the meeting, it's okay to request that the team reach such agreements. If you receive opposition from people not wanting to use agreements or norms, you may want to respond with something like, "It's important to create a safe space and to model positive communication for our students. I do find it helpful to remember that we should expect nothing less from ourselves than what we expect from our students. This can function as that simple reminder."

It also comes into play when that day comes in which the meeting suddenly hits stormy seas but we're able to right the ship by referring back to our team agreements that, for example, remind us we promised to speak one at a time and listen carefully to the ideas of others. Without having good charts for navigating, we're sunk!

Below are sample meeting agreements that I find helpful.

- Have your camera on (for virtual meetings).
- One person speaks at a time.
- Listen carefully to the ideas of others.
- Share your views willingly.
- Ask and welcome questions for clarification.
- Honor agreed time limits.
- Keep the meeting focused on the child.
- "Be hard on the problem and gentle with each other." (If you could only choose one, this is it, as first explained in *Getting to Yes* by Roger Fisher and William Ury.)
- Name any special needs.

Do not overlook that last point. Taking care of each other is important. Each of us has needs or requests that deserve consideration – because we all want to be good teammates. For example, we may ask that all cell phones be turned off during the meeting, but someone may have an elderly relative who is ill, another may have child-care issues, and someone else might have a job requirement to be "on call."

This is the opportunity for team members to say up front, "Today I need to leave my phone on vibrate, and if I see it's my family, I'll go outside and answer the call." By saying this at the beginning of the meeting, most likely we will all be supportive. But if a team member started texting or got up to take a phone call *without advance warning,* chances are we would think that person was being disrespectful. A special need can also be a time constraint, as in, "Sorry, but I can only stay twenty minutes because my sitter has to leave early today."

Each of us has needs or requests that deserve consideration.

Let's be clear about this too: "team agreements" are not limited to official group meetings. We should be just as agreeable *between* meetings when, for instance, we might be in a conversation with members of our team on a more casual or individual occasion. The right time and place for good communication is anytime and anywhere.

Let's be equally clear that meetings are not just about professional staff gatherings. A parent is every bit as important as any school official on an IEP team or in a community advisory council (CAC) meeting. And there may be only two people in a parent-teacher conference, but that too is a meeting, and it will benefit from having participants respect the sort of team agreements that apply to larger meetings.

With that in mind, consider how the first letter in IEP stands for *individualized* – which is to say, each meeting and each individual *in* the meeting, not only IEPs, is assumed to have equal standing. So it may be reasonable for professionals to initiate setting team agreements such as the list of sample agreements above "that I find helpful" (but maybe you don't), because some of the veteran staffers could be on hundreds of teams, while a parent may be on only one. Still, that one parent may have a unique need that should be added to the guidelines for their *individual* team.

Practicing This Skill

- Develop meeting agreements that work for your team. Get together with your colleagues. If you are in-person, bring a large poster board and some markers. Discuss and establish the team agreements that everyone should use at meetings. Maybe the sample above works for your team, or at least gets you started. Suggestion: once your poster board is set, laminate and post it in every meeting room. It helps to have visual reminders.

- Have a mock meeting with your colleagues and take turns being the facilitator in order to practice starting the meeting and getting consensus on the team agreements. Remember: *all* participants must agree to these protocols at the outset. Otherwise there is no way to enforce them later. Also, don't forget the value of each team member feeling a sense of ownership, so always ask if anyone has additions.
- Help make team agreements comfortable. For instance, if one of the agreements is "no cell phones," you could model this by conspicuously turning off your own phone as the meeting begins. And to support a "one person speaks at a time" rule, distribute extra paper and pens, as a reminder that instead of interrupting now, we can take notes for comments later.

"I" Messages Really Do Work

There I was, in Palm Beach, Florida, conducting professional development training for nonprofit administrators, and it was going great. Everyone was actively participating and had been open to learning new communication techniques. Then I came to the topic of "I" Messages and they immediately shut down. One of them proclaimed, "Oh, Marc, that stuff is a bunch of California woo-woo. It doesn't work on the East Coast."

I had to make my case, and I needed to "Use Objective (Legitimate) Criteria" (page 25). I suggested that they trust me on this, because the techniques – when used appropriately – absolutely work, which may be why "I" Message theory happens to be embedded in the curriculum at the Harvard School of Negotiation. (Invoking the Ivy League is a surefire defense against the dreaded woo-woo assault.)

The way that the "I" Message formula plays out in practice may be understood as follows.

Step 1: "I feel…" (Talk about your feelings.)
Step 2: "When…" (State the specific behavior.)
Step 3: "Because…" (Explain what happens to you.)
Step 4: "And what I *need* is…" (What makes the situation better.)

When we talk about difficult situations – those about which we have strong feelings – we need to be careful how we say things. We don't want to make the situation worse by prompting anger or confusion. We need to provide important information about ourselves quickly, clearly, and in a way that encourages the other person to work with us to find a solution.

Talk about yourself: about what you think, feel, need, and want. An example is, "I have a problem. I feel angry. I need more clarity from you about meeting times. I want to be able to plan the rest of my day. I think this problem is serious."

It's more effective to begin your sentences with "I" instead of "You."

Use neutral language, but be as specific as possible to convey how someone's actions made you feel. A sample *vague* statement is, "I can never count on you." A sample *specific* statement is, "I got angry when you forgot our meeting yesterday."

It's more effective to begin your sentences with "I" instead of "You." For instance, it's better to say, "I feel hurt and neglected when you don't let me know you'll be late for dinner," than if you say, "You don't care about me anymore. You are late on purpose to ruin my dinner and hurt my feelings."

State your positive intentions to resolve the conflict: something like, "This difficulty between us concerns me. I think if we sit down and talk, we can make things better. I'm willing to spend the time necessary to improve the situation." Similarly, tell the other person that you want to listen to their viewpoint, such as saying, "I realize we may each see this problem in a different way, and your point of view is important to me. I will take time to listen to all you have to say about it."

Practicing This Skill

- Try role-playing with one or two people you trust. Step 1: Everyone in your group will think about who they would say an "I" Message to. Take a few minutes and write it out. Once you've completed that, Step 2 calls on each person to share what they wrote and who they wrote it to. A scene partner is listening as if they were the person receiving the message. Step 3: Provide feedback. Ask, "How was it to receive this 'I'

Message?" and "Did my message put you on the defensive?" and "What can I do differently?"

- If you are part of a staff development or parent support group, take some time on this: Break up into pairs and have each person take a turn. Then reconvene the whole group and invite volunteers to share their "I" Messages. Remember, this "stuff" may be more art than science, but it works – and we can all learn from each other...even people from other coasts.

- "I" Messages should not stand alone. Once you feel comfortable with the "I" Messages, try using the formula for handling a challenging conversation (page 78) and practice incorporating several of the skills offered in this book. Rarely does just one skill suffice to handle a difficult situation.

Be Hard on the Problem and Gentle with Each Other

I'm not sure how many times a week I use this phrase, but it's a *lot*. It's a good one, though, and I often feel it can't be said often enough: "Be hard on the problem and gentle with each other." Isn't that a great concept?

When I conduct a mediation or facilitate a meeting, "Be hard on the problem and gentle with each other" (oops, I said it again) is at the top of the list of my suggested ground rules and norms for meetings. I wish I could take credit for coming up with this phrase, but I am nonetheless grateful that William Ury and Roger Fisher popularized it in their book *Getting to Yes.*

Out of all the team agreements mentioned earlier (page 9), this is the most important, especially if excellent problem-solving techniques and behaviors are virtues that we want to model for our students or children.

We certainly do not want to be hard on the problem *and* hard on each other. Here's an example of that. A parent comes into a meeting yelling, "My child is not staying on task and keeps running out into the hall. You are not helping my child learn and can't even get him to stay in the classroom. So incompetent!"

An example of being hard on the problem and gentle with each other is for that same parent to say, calmly but forthrightly, "My child is having difficulty staying on task, and I am also concerned about his safety, as he sometimes leaves the classroom. Let's look at what's going on so we can make some adjustments." That approach will surely gain agreement from the district members of the team about the seriousness of the problem, without putting them on the defensive. It seems that everyone in the room can be sensible, collaborative, and otherwise ready to roll up their sleeves and get to work on a fair solution. In other words, be ready to be hard on the problem.

By committing to be hard on the problem and gentle with each other, we establish partnerships that are mutually supportive instead of contentious. We're less likely to "take sides" because we recognize we're all on the student's side – and that's a side deserving of our best attention and effort. It keeps us focused on the important issues and interests, and less on distractions and personalities. Put that all together and we become – as a team and individually – our best and most effective selves. Not to mention, we set a great example.

So it bears repeating: Be hard on the problem and gentle with each other.

Practicing This Skill

- Think about the last challenging conversation you had. Were you hard on the problem and gentle with the others in the conversation? How might you have been too hard on the person? How were you hard on the problem?
- Next time you are in a meeting, ask for one of the team agreements to be, "Be hard on the problem and gentle with each other." I guarantee you there will be people nodding their heads in agreement and thinking you're brilliant for suggesting it.
- Consider putting the phrase "Be hard on the problem and gentle with each other" on a wall poster for meeting rooms, or as stickers meant for laptops and day planners. Maybe even T-shirts. (Picture them becoming a team jersey at PTA or staff meetings!)

Avoiding Distractions

We usually think of a distraction as a relatively minor and momentary setback, a slight detour from the road. On the other hand, let's say you're driving on that road and are distracted by a noisy passenger or a funny billboard and, in that moment, the car ahead of you makes a sudden stop. That's when you learn a hard lesson about the not-so-slight difference between *distraction* and *destruction*. So, how does this relate to us here? Read on.

A survey revealed that the main reason parents file due-process complaints involving Individualized Education Programs (IEPs) is that they did not feel heard. Feeling disrespected really stings, and one common source of it in the relationship between parents and schools is the distracting school environment itself. Let's at least recognize that this is unintentional, but better yet, let's do more to minimize distractions in order to have more positive and productive school-parent meetings.

Life for most of us can be hectic, confusing, unpredictable, and stressful. Those descriptions also apply to a lot of schools: the environment where most parent-teacher conferences, staff meetings, IEPs, and other meetings take place. When a conversation deserves undivided attention (and don't they all?), your first consideration should be to find a location that presents minimum distractions.

Imagine we are in an IEP meeting for your child, or your student, and that it takes place in the child's classroom. During the meeting, other students are streaming in and out of the room. The teacher is constantly interrupted by questions, and may be simultaneously putting away supplies or organizing papers, and thus making little eye contact. At the same time, the administrator is called out on the walkie-talkie to go to the front office, and one of the service providers is texting away.

Of course, the distractions could also come from the family: parents taking work calls on a cell phone, or the child who keeps popping into the classroom asking, "When can we go home?"

Avoiding distractions may seem like a no-brainer, but it really does need your conscious attention – and a plan – as soon as the agreement is made to have a serious talk. That's important whether it be a formal meeting for an IEP or an informal conversation between parent and teacher. Not only the location you choose but also the commitment you make to be available as an active listener (without that cell phone or walkie-talkie) will play a critical role in determining the tone and outcome of your meeting.

> Avoiding distractions needs conscious attention and a plan as soon as the agreement is made to have a serious talk.

So, where do you find a distraction-free environment? Ideally there would be a comfortable room with four walls and a functional thermostat: someplace conducive to private, uninterrupted conversation. If you have such a room on your campus or at your business, you're lucky. Just be sure to promptly book it for a reasonable amount of time! In many cases, however, the solution is not so handy. When I am working at a school site, I sometimes recommend having a conversation out on the yard or in the lunch area when students are not around.

In meetings, we need to anticipate what our distractions may be, and call them out up front. Here are some examples. If you're a site administrator and your walkie-talkie might go off, you might explain in advance that "I'm on call, and I need to leave my walkie-talkie on in case there's an emergency on campus. If it goes off, I'll have to excuse myself. But I'm going to put it by my feet so it won't be a distraction."

Another example: A team member is the caregiver for an elderly relative. She might explain at the beginning of the meeting, "I'm going to leave my phone on vibrate, and I may have to step out if I get a call from my house."

Virtual meetings have their own set of distraction traps, such as a tendency to find participants multitasking. Also, if you're a parent or anybody being linked in from home (maybe with children running around, barking dogs, package deliveries, a sketchy internet connection, and so on), please forewarn the rest of the meeting participants at the beginning of the meeting. Most likely they will accept and support these team members and their special needs.

Remember, if they don't say anything beforehand and just take the call or leave the room without any explanation, chances are the others will think they are rude and disrespectful. It's the sort of thing that leads to parents feeling they should file for due process.

We should also turn briefly to another sort of distraction. It's more of a self-imposed distraction. Let's call it a "brain hiccup." Everybody has them now and then. You tune out of a meeting for no better reason than your mind wanders or gets interrupted by something else that pulls your attention away.

Certainly this will happen less often if you enter the meeting well-rested, prepared, and with a conscious effort to concentrate on the business at hand. But if it happens, understand that it will be annoying to the others, and by far the best thing you can do is catch it, own it, apologize for it, and humbly ask for a conversation "rewind." Trying to bluff your way out of it will probably only make you look more foolish and less responsible.

Similarly, if you spot someone else in the meeting who is apparently preoccupied with something irrelevant – or maybe even dozing off – it may seem polite to ignore it, but you're better off calling it out. However, be gentle and perhaps show some good-natured humor that acknowledges that we all do it once in a while. Use something like, "I can tell some of us are zoning out right now. Would this be a good time to take a little stretch break? Then we can recap a bit of where we left off, and continue this good discussion."

No matter what, there will always be some type of unavoidable distractions that come up. The important thing is, to the best of our ability, to anticipate and alert the others to interruptions we know might occur and, in all cases, catch it and correct it, the sooner the better.

Practicing This Skill

Step 1: Grab flip chart paper and some markers. Then, with a trusted friend or colleague, write down as many examples as you can recall of distractions you've come across in recent meetings. When doing this exercise, it is important to evaluate both in-person and virtual meetings.

Step 2: With all these distractions fresh in your mind, write down what you can do – moving forward – to ensure the most successful and distraction-free meeting. What does the room setup look like? What type of team meeting agreements need to be said in the beginning of the meeting? (See page 9.) For in-person meetings, does a sign need to be placed outside the room to let folks know that a meeting is in progress? For virtual meetings, what agreements need to be established that may be different from meetings that are in person?

Separating Interests
from Positions

A mother marches into the principal's office and declares, "You must immediately transfer my daughter to Mr. Smith's class because she's not learning in Mrs. Jones's class." This is the parent's *position*. But is it her *interest*? The difference – could make all the difference.

A position, whether it is "ours" or "theirs," aims for a particular result and usually grabs our focus, especially when it takes the form of a demand. But no matter how forcefully the position is stated, we are wise to identify and understand the more subtle interest that motivates it.

Otherwise, giving in to the position may not resolve the issue at all. After all, if your child says, "My stomach hurts," there could be countless reasons why. So, before considering the evidence suggested by all those candy wrappers under the bed, would you charge off to the ER and insist they remove your child's appendix? (Then maybe cheer up the recovering young patient with a favorite candy bar…?)

Getting back to the parent-principal exchange – the mother's intention could be straightforward: to replace the daughter's inadequate teacher with a better one. Or, among other possibilities, it might be that the parent is simply not receiving enough communication from the otherwise excellent Mrs. Jones. This conversation with the principal may well result in moving the student to Mr. Smith's class, but hopefully that decision would've followed careful consideration and not just caving in to parental pressure.

The parent could have set a better tone in the first place by approaching the principal with something more like, "Thanks for taking time to meet me about my concerns with my daughter's teacher. I'd like her to receive as much value from the class as possible. Can you help me?" (For other effective conversation-starters, see "The Art of the Question," page 5.)

On the other hand, what if the principal in this scenario responded defensively to the parent, and with similar force? That's not good either. A better approach all around would be to engage in communication techniques not meant to win this argument, but rather to recognize and hopefully remedy the parent's underlying concerns, which could even be such basic human needs as

Think issues, not services

security, economic well-being, a sense of belonging, recognition and appreciation, and control over one's life.

Keep your antenna up to spot such motives, being sensitive to the possibility that when positions escalate to the level of demands, it may just be that the interests are overheated by deeper concerns or fears. That awareness might prevent those nightmare meetings where, right from the start, some are shouting, "I want it!" and the others are shouting back, "You can't have it!" After all, it only makes matters worse if the "it" that cannot be resolved has needlessly become the *only* issue discussed.

That doesn't mean it's wrong to bring suggestions to the meeting. Just allow – even encourage – others to offer suggestions of their own. Let's appreciate that each of us has our own experience, perspective, and imagination to bring to this partnership, and nobody involved is more important than the student. Your idea may be great, but it could be improved with some added tweaks that hadn't occurred to you. And yes, there can even be entirely better solutions than yours, if you are open to seeing it, for the sake of the student.

The point I really want to make is that everyone around the table should be speaking interests and not positions. It's my professional fantasy that instead of, "I demand speech services for my child," a parent would say, "I'm concerned that no one understands my son. I want him to learn how to advocate for himself. I want my child to have friends." Surely good team members would respond sympathetically to those interests, and would willingly extend their hearts and minds to do right by that student.

By coming from the interests perspective, we set the ideal tone and focus for all participants so that we may open an opportunity for the school team and parents to have a caring discussion about all the reasonable ways to address a concern. It is the truest course to the best possible outcome.

A brilliant colleague and friend (who for years has been in these meetings from the perspectives of both a parent and a professional) has summed up perfectly how best to identify the actual concerns and best resolve them. Her advice: "Think issues, not services!"

Practicing This Skill

- For each "position" statement below, do two things. First: write underlying "interests" that could be motivating it. Second: as a response to the statement, write a question you would use in order to bring out the underlying interest.

  - **Parent:** I want Mary moved to Bob's class by Monday. He's a more creative teacher.
  - **Office staffer to administrator:** Arlene and Joan gossip all the time. I hate it, and I don't want to work here anymore!
  - **Parent:** I do not agree with your policy, so I won't sign the form.
  - **Teacher to parent:** Your child doesn't belong in my class.
  - **Speech therapist:** I have a caseload that keeps increasing while the other therapists have caseloads that stay the same or decrease. I can't do this anymore!
  - **Parent:** I want a one-to-one aide for my child.

- Share a recent experience in which you or someone in a meeting with you made a demand that indicated a deeper concern. How did that go? What, if anything, was done to handle the situation? What could have been done better?

Use Objective (Legitimate) Criteria

I get no commission or any other reward, except great satisfaction, for recommending *Getting to Yes: Negotiating Agreement Without Giving In* by Roger Fisher and William Ury. It's an easy-to-read and practical book that emphasizes preparation for interest-based negotiations, and it makes a particularly strong case for the value of bringing as many objective criteria as possible to a negotiation.

That's how to earn "legitimacy" (credibility, respect, stature, and so on), which is especially effective in situations involving advocacy for our children and students. Their importance to us is understandably personal, but feelings are not evidence. Emotions can cloud objectivity, and expressing those emotions more than presenting our evidence can cause others to take us less seriously and thus be dismissive of our cause.

Here is one of the biggest mistakes I've seen repeatedly during my years as both a state mediator and in private practice: People make requests based on feelings, instinct, and gut reactions rather than reasoned, impartial factors and documentation.

Consider this example.

During an Individualized Education Program (IEP) team meeting, a father is asked by the district representative to explain why he requested an added hour of speech services for his daughter. He replies, "Because I'm having difficulty understanding what she is saying."

Or how about this dialogue exchange?

Resource teacher: Great news! Mike is doing so well that I recommend to the IEP team here that we decrease his support to consultation only.

The mom: Wow, that is surprising news! Tell me how you know he's doing so well?

Resource teacher: Well, Mike is passing all his classes.

Can you see how these two requests could lack legitimacy? Both the parent and the teacher might be absolutely correct. However, neither one provided supporting facts.

Before making a change in the IEP service, the team members need to receive and agree on objective information. In the above case with the dad, it's simply not enough for him to tell the IEP team that he wants more speech services because he can't understand his daughter. He'd be far more persuasive if he included a professional assessment report by a speech and language pathologist, or corroborating testimony by the daughter's teacher, current speech therapist, and other service providers.

In the second example, there could be several other reasons why Mike is passing his classes, including his reliance on the very support that would disappear if the teacher's request is granted.

Setting aside an educational context, imagine you are negotiating with a car dealer. What compelling objective criteria can you bring that both you and the dealer may factor into determining a fair price? Did you say, "Kelley Blue Book?" If yes, you get the gist of it, and get bonus points if you also thought of citing published prices from other dealers.

Some more topical examples:

- If you want better communication with your child's teacher, you might bring in a sample communication log used by a previous school team.
- Maybe the district has a specific protocol on how its employees communicate with parents.

- You might ask the teacher, "What's your preferred way to communicate?" or find out if the teacher has office hours.

From the school's side, it could be that you want better communication from the parent, or you want your student to come to school on time. The legitimacy you can bring in might be documented via student grades, district attendance policies, and perhaps specific curricula that the student is missing by not being in school.

The point is, by insisting on objective criteria (like the Kelley Blue Book or the posted attendance policies), it helps to take emotion out of the conversation. In my role as a neutral party, I want everyone to get whatever they want – but you'd better have objective material to back up your requests.

Whether buying a car, requesting a promotion, or seeking special education support services for a child, your command of credible, objective criteria is essential to getting what you want. So from here on out, when making decisions or stating your case, insist on the Kelley Blue Book equivalent.

Practicing This Skill

- See the meeting prep sheet in appendix 1 (page 89).
- Think about a recent negotiation you had that went poorly. What objective information could you have brought that would have made the conversation go better?
- Think about a recent negotiation you had that went well. What was the objective information that made it work?
- Prepare for the next challenging conversation or negotiation that you're going to have with a colleague, teacher, or parent. Write down some objective information that you could bring to the conversation that will help you reach an agreement.

Don't Argue Mentally

When was the last time you were voicing some disagreement without really listening to the opposing viewpoint? Come on; we've all done it. You enter the conversation, debate, or negotiation and then tune out. Why? Because you already decided you know what that person's position is, and you prefer your own opinions. You're not even hearing their words because you're too busy calculating what words *you* are going to say next. What you're doing – inside your closed mind – is stating that you are entirely right, and they are entirely wrong. When that arrogant tone surfaces in the conversation (or meeting!), are you making more points or more enemies?

Take me, for instance. Yes I, Mr. Communicator and conflict resolution expert, was recently on the phone speaking with a relative about politics (rule number 1 of what one should never discuss with kin). Sure enough, as soon as he began talking, I was already shaking my head and plotting my witty retorts. I was thinking to myself, "He doesn't know anything, and I am going to teach him." So I devised my arguments while he was speaking, and envisioned how humbled he would feel when I unleashed my superior wisdom upon him. Of course, my lack of attention meant I missed every point he was making.

Eventually I did own up and apologize (see "The Role of Apology," page 53). We agreed once again not to discuss politics, an agreement that I reckon will last at least a couple of election cycles. If I had been more open to his views, might he have been more open to mine? Would either of us have persuaded the other to reconsider or modify their position, if not reverse it? The answer is a resounding "Who knows?" But as it stood, we dug in our heels and never budged an inch.

So what about you? Reflect on a recent difficult conversation of your own in which the other person was speaking while you were "in your head" crafting a sharp response instead of thoughtfully being "present."

Maximize alternatives; minimize assumptions

Perhaps your example was something like a discussion at a staff meeting or during an Individualized Education Program (IEP) team meeting, when parents were requesting additional speech services for their child. Or maybe it was a school psychologist telling parents of concerns about their child being able to stay on task.

Some people are highly experienced in this setting, such as the school psychologist who regularly conducts IEP meetings, whereas the parents may see that as their home-field advantage. For them the meeting is not at all routine. It is an intimidating and momentous event, the outcome of which means nothing less than their child's future. Each, in their own way, would benefit from the advice of "Don't argue mentally."

Veteran school officials may feel they've "heard it all before" and arrive armed with standardized policies and precedents. Maybe they've even gone so far as to come with a draft IEP outcome in hand, before hearing a single word proposed by the parents. Similarly, maybe the parents are so stressed by the unfamiliar process that they've been playing out scenarios in their heads, all of which assume the school is their enemy. In effect, they have convinced themselves to expect the meeting to be a nasty uphill battle, and have rehearsed it accordingly.

Don't get me wrong: preparation is not a bad thing. Of course research, experience, and organization have value, but so does an open mind. There is a difference between contingency plans and predetermined ones. Maximize alternatives; minimize assumptions. Do your best to enter the meeting without pet plans, demands, or any other mind-set that will lead you to take matters too personally.

Instead, come prepared with topics, issues, and interests that can be described and discussed fairly by all parties – parties who mutually agree on their shared mission to serve the student's needs. That approach is far more likely to bring about a harmonious result.

Here is an actual illustration. A special-needs child had trouble with handwriting. The parent request or suggestion (not a demand) was for the school to provide voice-activated software. The teacher wonders (not argues) if there might be a better measure taken besides providing costly equipment that could disrupt an entire classroom and which doesn't accomplish a long-term solution.

This approach led to a thoughtful conversation and open brainstorming from everyone in the meeting, and resulted in an alternative, namely to teach the child keyboarding. It provided an immediate and practical course of action and enabled the student to gain a normative lifelong skill.

When people speak, they rightly expect you to listen, and your ability to listen with respectful open-mindedness will usually gain *their* respect and open-mindedness. So let's improve our ability to consider what is being said while they are saying it, not before. Then we're likely to be given the same courtesy. It is the smart, productive, and right thing to do.

Practicing This Skill

- Use the question! If you're in a conversation where you feel you're slipping and already tuning out so that you can prepare your devastating retort, halt. Ask a nonthreatening question (see "The Art of the Question," page 5), wait for the response, and allow your mind to slow down so it can re-engage and listen to the other party.
- Pay attention to yourself, specifically your brain. When you find yourself arguing in your head while someone else is speaking, pause. Trust that you'll get your turn to speak and hopefully be heard.

React to the Idea, Not the Person

Sometimes we unfortunately pay more attention to the personality of an individual than to what the person is saying. That's especially true when these people are highly emotional or have dominating egos. We can find ourselves similarly distracted or intimidated by other external factors, such as physicality, professional status, educational background, renown in the field, and so forth. So how can we overcome these situations, and keep the conversation focused on the ideas and interests of the individual, rather than focusing on personality, appearance, title, or behavior?

Let me see if I can give you a good example. I was working with a single mother who has two children with disabilities. They just entered into a new school district and were unhoused. This is a mom who clearly had a lot on her plate, including some issues of her own. Speaking with her, it was very easy to get sidetracked.

When she complained about her old school district and expressed anger and frustration at how she was treated there, I would acknowledge it by saying, "It sounds like you and your kids had a really negative experience at your last school district." She'd answer, "Yes, that's true." I might then ask her, "One of the reasons you've come to the new district is the hope of getting a fresh start; is that right?" She'd answer in the affirmative. I continued to use questions from "The Art of the Question" chapter (page 5), such as, "How will you know if you and your children are getting a fresh start?" and "What will it look like to see improved communication between you and your child's school?"

I maintained this approach by saying something like, "I would like you to have this fresh start. You would benefit from a supportive environment with a good communication plan among the adults." Even then, her response could be to scream, "Marc, they're killing me. I don't have time to look for a job because I'm spending all my time advocating for my kids!" Nonetheless, I would calmly say, "So getting a program where you know your children's needs are being met is important to you. I'd like to work with you and the school team so that you can have that."

Conversations like this would happen over time – and many felt like repeat performances – but it was important to stay consistent and avoid being drawn into emotional detours. The key was to stay focused on the interests and react to her ideas, not her personality.

At the same time, I was getting feedback from the school part of the team that this parent was disrespectful, came into the office shouting, and constantly sent emails accusing district staff of wrongdoing. So I'd ask them, "What would you like to see happen?"

You see, it's important also to have *them* focus more on the ideas and interests than on the personalities. I might explain to the district staff how important it is for everyone to come up with a communication plan between the school and the parent, so that the parent is getting the information she needs, and so that staff members likewise feel respected. Keep in mind that everyone in this dynamic has interests that need acknowledging, especially the children.

This skill is by far one of this book's harder ones to master. I've been in this field a long time, and I still struggle with focusing on the interests and ideas rather than on that strong personality. And although my example above concerns a parent, believe me, there are many examples where someone on the school team has an intrusive ego, or another one has distracting mannerisms, or the student being discussed is the child of a prominent school official, and so on. Speaking of distractions and VIPs, I'm thinking of the colleague who had great difficulty keeping proper focus during meetings involving the special-needs child of a highly involved parent who also happened to be a popular and charismatic TV star!

Whoever else is in the meeting – no matter how famous, belligerent, influential, insulting, friendly, unattractive, obstructive, inspiring, demanding, disturbing, you name it – you are there too, and the issue at hand is a child in need of your best attention. One of those distracting others may turn out to be the source of a worthwhile idea. Don't miss it because you were distracted by the less important factor of a forceful personality.

On the contrary, you should assume those good ideas will come forth at any moment, and that you're going to be the one who recognizes and nurtures them. You do this by keeping your own demeanor consistent, your focus clear, your mind open, and your communication always forward-looking.

Practicing This Skill

- Think of a recent situation where the conversation or negotiation shut down because personality, position, or physical demeanor got in the way. As you reflect back, can you identify the interests of this person? What can you do to reopen the dialogue with the intention of focusing on the interests and needs? Be sure to look for any interests *in common.*

- At your next IEP or other student-focused meeting, zero in on identifying the interests and needs of each team member. Anytime you find yourself distracted from this goal, be gentle on yourself (remember to breathe) and go back to focusing on what the individual is saying.

- Get together with a few people you trust and try role-playing. Imagine that you are all participants in an IEP team meeting. Choose someone to be a high-personality teacher, parent, aide, administrator, or specialist, and have them come up with a valid concern or request. As this individual is speaking, focus only on what they are saying. After completing the role-play, it is important to debrief with all the participants and to verify if the interests were accurately identified.

Time to Brake, Break, and Breathe

*I*n the middle of the school term, it can feel like you're barely holding on, awaiting the next break. Are you familiar with that funk? Or maybe your doldrums are not limited to the midyear blues. In any case, whenever it strikes, I want you to ease off the gas pedal for a moment, glance into the mirror, and answer honestly: How is it going? Is it one of those times when you should turn to "the three B's" to help you stay on course?

Brake. This refers to the psychological technique of telling ourselves to stop putting negative energy into what's driving us. (I'm not suggesting making external changes.) When we're busy and most likely wearing multiple hats, it's natural to rev up to overdrive mode. But when we do that, we miss the scenery passing by us – and perhaps some important road signs. We lose sight of the why, what, and who of our jobs. And we lose awareness of how we feel, and how others perceive us. We don't even know if we're communicating in ways that are being understood, and we're definitely impaired in our ability to understand other perspectives. Braking allows us to stop building up anger, resentment, frustration, or whatever else we might be feeling that may be taking us off track. Putting on the brakes allows us to take those necessary breaks.

Break. This can be a five-minute "I need some air" break or a "Let's sleep on it" break. What matters is taking time to comprehend and process things such as what has just been said in a meeting, as well as to gather our thoughts so that we can communicate in a positive, productive way. Bear in mind that a break usually involves other people, so it is important to get agreement on how long it will last – ten minutes, one day, a week.... The added benefit to a break is that it allows us a healthy step away, to let us breathe different air.

Breathe. If we had to put on the brakes, chances are we weren't properly breathing. Working in special education and having children or students with disabilities can be challenging and emotional. For parents, it's also personal. No matter who we are, we should remember to breathe. As I write this, it seems so simple: "Don't forget to breathe!" Duh, right? True enough, but I chose this topic because I too can forget to "Brake, Break, and Breathe," especially during certain times of the year. But I know that when I force myself to do it, I become calmer, more grounded, and open to continuing that tough conversation. Try it – it works.

Practicing This Skill

- Feeling anxious before a tough meeting? Set a timer for five minutes and then use that time to simply breathe. It will relax you, ground you, and open you to being your most effective.
- Focus on the positives and show appreciation for what is working. A "win" can be as simple as getting everyone together for an IEP meeting, or telling a teacher you appreciate the way she communicates.

Celebrate and Take a Break

*T*hroughout the year, the school calendar provides district staff and families "breaks" (at least from each other!). Whether you are a parent, student, teacher, administrator, service provider, or other staff member, those are times to make those breaks even better by using them to celebrate. This involves two "skills":

Celebrate. District staff and parents: You both need to reflect on the year and look at your achievements. How have you been able to support your students? If you are a parent, what is at least one new way that you are working with your child's school? If you are a district employee, what are new ways you have worked with some of your most challenging families or fellow employees? Maybe you have made some positive systematic changes. If so, celebrate them!

There is no such thing as success too small or too "boring." Heck, it could be that you have built new trust with a family, and now the parents are saying hello to their child's teachers, when before there was no greeting at all. From that little triumph could grow huge progress.

Take a Break. So now that we have reflected on the accomplishments of the past year, it's time for some well-earned R&R. We all need rejuvenation. So get away, whether it's a "stay-cation" or venturing somewhere far and exotic. Simply blocking out time to take a weekly walk on the beach can work wonders, as can escaping to your imagination at a local movie theater.

I offer this skill in hopes that you will celebrate your successes over the past year and take a break so that you can return fresh and optimistic for the next school year. I look forward to our continuing work together and supporting families and districts in any way I can. You know, it feels great to say optimistic things like that. Try it and see!

Practicing This Skill

- Reflect on the past year, or even the last month, and make a list of your accomplishments. If you are saying to yourself that you don't have any, I really don't believe you! Reach out to your support team if you need some help with this; I'm sure they have some great ideas.
- Take out your summer calendar and block out time to relax and revive. It doesn't matter if your plans are grand or modest. What matters is that you get some mental time off and have that to look forward to. If you are staying local, make a list of nearby things that make you happy and that enable you to rest up. No excuses! We have *lots* of free activities available in our communities.

Modeling the Common Core

Before graduating high school, students are expected to have the ability to:

- prepare for and participate effectively in a range of collaborative conversations
- come to the conversation prepared
- be collegial
- elaborate the discussion
- refine ideas and understanding

These excellent communication skills are built into the "Common Core State Standards Initiative," used by schools throughout the country since 2010. It's a curricular priority – and mandate – right up there with reading, writing, and math. We're talking about necessary tools for having a successful adult life. It only makes sense for students to expect their teachers, counselors, and others to have these Common Core skills as well.

So we're posing this question to school personnel (and parents too): How are you modeling these standards for your students? It's not necessarily an easy thing to do.

It's one thing to teach math and reading. You start with "1, 2, 3" and "A, B, C," then go from there. But where is the primer for teaching communication, cooperation, and teamwork? I heartily agree with Common Core that these skills are essential for life after high school. In fact, the work we do at Purchin Consulting – including providing this workbook – pretty much mirrors that goal.

It would be a shame if those "language arts" expectations were treated as a lesser part of the curriculum when, in fact, it could be said it's in your job description, whether as a school official or a parent! Hopefully everyone in this partnership will recognize and uphold *all* Common Core standards. As an extra note: using these communication skills and tips can be a plus when you're in situations, such as a school-parent conference, and want to do right by your student. Nobody wants those meetings to fail. Keeping this book handy could be very helpful.

> Using these communication skills can be a plus to do right by your student.

None of us wants conflict and dysfunction in the relationship between school and family – or any other important relationship. Yet there are ways to deal with setbacks if they happen, and even better, there are ways to avoid them in the first place. Either way, the key is to learn the same techniques used by the best communicators. They are the ones known for their ability to understand what is most important and to work well with others to resolve issues. Now scroll up to the top of this chapter and reread the five points. It's right on target!

For sure, each point deserves closer attention, further explanation, and some tips or exercises to build up your preparation and confidence, but it's well worth the effort. And now that you have this book in front of you, let it serve as a kind of instruction manual.

Think about another Common Core subject – mathematics – and how learning it calls for descriptions of problems, methods to solve them, and exercises to sharpen your discipline and increase your ability to apply those concepts to solving future problems. The same goes for this skill set. As your own communication abilities improve, your job performance and relationships will improve too. And if you model that for children, it will be a super-satisfying achievement.

Practicing This Skill

- Use this Common Core directive as a perfect excuse for your team to meet. At that meeting, post the five required standards, and then go through them one by one – as a unified group – and discuss how individuals and the team as a whole are doing, and could be doing better. Here again are those communication skills we are being counted on to instill in all students:
  - prepare for and participate effectively in a range of collaborative conversations
  - come to the conversation prepared
  - be collegial
  - elaborate the discussion
  - refine ideas and understanding
- Pick any chapter in this book and practice the skills emphasized in it. All of them are directly relevant to modeling these Common Core standards.

"Direct, Honest, Respectful"

Successful communication and effective Alternative Dispute Resolution (ADR) is more art than science. Good ideas can come in many forms and from many sources. From the start, I have emphasized that "good ADR" is not about mediators like me, but rather about building a culture. Within the ADR world, if something is working well or someone has an amazing skill, we want to borrow it, adopt it, and use it. There's no need to reinvent the wheel. We all learn from each other and can start using these skills in our work environment to help move things forward, for the benefit of everyone.

When I had the opportunity to help create and develop an ADR program within a large regional association of twelve school districts and twenty-two charter schools, one of the things I implemented right away was an Alternative Dispute Resolution Skill Recognition Award. The award was an opportunity for us to spotlight an individual who introduced a tool or technique that has been successful in preventing conflict situations – or for positively working through them.

One of the winners, nominated by a teacher, was the mantra "Direct, Honest, Respectful," created by a school principal who posted those words in the conference room where Individualized Educational

Program (IEP) meetings take place. You couldn't miss it, and it served as a loud-and-clear everyday reminder of the manner in which staff, administrators, students, and parents agreed to communicate with each other.

We all know that three little words can mean a lot. That's certainly true of "Direct, Honest, Respectful." Those are watchwords to live by on any campus or district office, don't you agree?

Of course, it may take time and care to build the trust and safety necessary for us to be direct. And maybe it's even difficult for many to be consistently honest. Being respectful, however, is a worthy approach right from the start. Before being direct, consider the perspectives of those you are engaging (see the chapter on "Separating Interests from Positions," page 22) and make sure you've taken time to ask thoughtful questions ("The Art of the Question," page 5) and to actively listen. For that matter, a refresher on the skill about "I" Messages (page 13) could be useful here too.

Practicing This Skill

- Think of a tough situation and make a list of ways you can address it by being more direct, honest, and respectful.
- With trusted individuals, practice being direct, honest, and respectful. Ask for feedback. How did it come across? Are you too abrupt? What could be different? Remember to apply the communication techniques explained in this book.
- Do you offer an award for ADR or positive communication? If not, think about establishing one. Conflict resolution is tough work, and we need opportunities to highlight what is working, as well as to show (and receive) appreciation for improving our skills. We all learn from each other, and it's a great feeling to be recognized. Parents and students should of course be eligible for such honors. See the sample ADR nomination form in appendix 2 (page 90).

Say Hello to the Elephant in the Room

When there is an obvious situation or subject that can't be ignored but no one wants to talk about it, why do we refer to it as "the elephant in the room?" Maybe we should change the term to "the hot fudge sundae in the room." If we did that, no one would avoid it (except maybe dieters). Okay, let's not get distracted. Getting distracted and veering off topic is an easy enough trap to fall into, when what we need to do instead is get to the point!

Yes, an elephant is a huge attention-grabber, which is all the more reason to make a point of acknowledging that elephant right up front. The thing to do is walk right up to it and shake hands – and perhaps do so by using those strategies we talked about in "The Art of the Question" (page 5).

Think of an Individualized Education Program (IEP) meeting when the advocate walks into the room and the tension immediately rises. Or the district employee who arrives frantic and obviously not grounded for the meeting at hand. Perhaps this elephant is that the principal has another meeting to attend but doesn't want to admit the time constraint.

Again, we need to pull out those question strategies to see how we might get back on track. If we don't do this, it can make the meeting increasingly uncomfortable. Perhaps we should pull this person outside and say something like, "I was wondering if I can check in with you. I notice you may have a lot on your plate. How can I support you?"

Recently, in a virtual meeting, the advocate appeared on screen not wearing a shirt. This was a clear elephant in the room. I wasn't at this meeting, but my colleague who was facilitating debriefed me about it. I asked, "Did anyone say anything?" She said, "No, everyone did their best to ignore it." I see why that would be uncomfortable to bring up.

> Acknowledging the "elephant" to yourself is not enough, because if you're thinking about it, you can be sure other people are too.

I can't say there's a right way to address the elephant, and we all have different styles, but as a facilitator, if something is distracting, I need to address it. It needs to be done in a way that is perceived as kind and respectful. I would never confront this advocate in front of the full team. Had I been there, I might have called for a short break, and in a breakout room, I would have checked in by saying, "I just wanted to check in with you, to make sure you knew your camera was on, and that you're not wearing a shirt."

I was recently assisting a family and a school at an IEP meeting. The elephant in the room was a strong disagreement regarding a student's intellectual disability eligibility. The parents believed that the district part of the team had prejudged the issue. Instead of ignoring the controversy or waiting until later in the meeting to bring it up, I encouraged the parents to state their concern right off the bat.

Everyone already knew this was a point of contention, so bringing it up in the beginning of the meeting allowed the entire team to take a breath and go through the legal steps of the IEP without being on non-stop pins and needles. If they did not discuss this up front, the elephant would have stayed in the room for hours, likely stressing and agitating all members of the team.

Even better than at the start of the meeting would be prior to the meeting, so that team members (parents and district alike) would be able to communicate their concerns and prepare for the eligibility issue. It might even have been stated as an actual agenda item to be discussed at the meeting.

There are many kinds of elephants. In any of these situations, it is important to take a break and check in. Acknowledging it to yourself is not enough, because if you're thinking about it, you can be sure other people are too. Sometimes we have to take one for the team and say it out loud. A shirtless speaker could be shrugged off, but when we have something important to discuss and we're prevented from doing that effectively, all because of a major distraction or pretending a serious controversy will go unnoticed? Nope. We have to talk about it and – as safely as we can – get that elephant out of our room.

Practicing This Skill

- Next time you're in a meeting, pay attention to unspecified uncomfortable feelings. Ask yourself, "What's happening? Is there an elephant in the room? If so, do I need to check in with the team? Does someone need to say it out loud?"
- After the meeting, debrief with a trusted team member about that elephant. If it wasn't spoken about, decide if there needs to be follow-up communication, as the elephant may have distracted participants from hearing important points and in other ways.
- Compare "elephant in the room" experiences you have had – even if they have nothing to do with school-parent situations. What was the elephant of your story? How did it distract or undermine the situation? What did you do about it? What might you have done better? Do other team members have opinions about how they might've shooed your elephant out the door? Sharing stories can be a fun team-builder and, in this case, also instructive.

New Term, New 'Tude

*I*n conflict resolution, it often helps to find ways to start fresh. There's frequently a need for people to put the past behind them in order to rebuild trust, or establish it once and for all after prior attempts faltered. For those of us doing this work in educational contexts, we are fortunate to have a ready-made opportunity to refresh our attitudes and energies. It's called "August" or "September," depending on your school district.

The new school year is a natural and wonderful occasion for everyone to get off on the right foot: parents, teachers, and school district officials alike. It's always an exciting time, brimming with potential. It's opening day when everybody's favorite team is tied for first place. It's our annual shot at a honeymoon period, when optimism and good will are most abundant. In other words, it's that moment when we have our greatest prospects for breakthroughs, for progress, for establishing positive precedents, and ultimately for gaining successful outcomes.

With so much promise in the fall air, the one thing we must not do is blow the chance. If you are entering this new term still dragging around last year's baggage – mistrust, grudges, and the like – then you are surely setting yourself up for failure. And that means failure for your child or student. So, for everyone's sake, do whatever you can to rinse away any lingering bad tastes in your mouth.

This is a prime time to call upon your supports, especially those people you can connect with to practice these skills together: partners such as teachers, program specialists, and parent support groups. Also feel free to drop in (online) for regular virtual office hours at Purchin Consulting. These are open to all (and fun too!), offered to support whatever will advance the ability of your student or child to learn and be safe. Our chances to achieve that goal are far better when we work in partnership – and get off to the right start.

A Closing Thought

The start of a new term may offer the most obvious opportunities to rededicate yourself to the important work ahead, but the *spirit* of new beginnings is worthwhile any time of year. Remember that you are part of an ongoing team and that all members of that team are mutually dedicated to supporting children who need them – throughout the year. Therefore, it is always essential to nurture positive relationships and open communication between staff members and parents. Your support network includes the teacher, principal, special education coordinator or director, program specialists, and parent liaisons in your district. Use them; you are not alone. Together, you can have a great year!

Practicing This Skill

- Welcome each other to the new school year. Just as we want the students to have a fresh start, the adults need a fresh start too.
- If you're a teacher, let parents know the best form and style of communication with you: phone calls, emails, walk-ins, communication logs, and so on. If you're a parent, respect this request, but if the method honestly doesn't work for you, come up with something together that does.
- Parents, create a "one page" about your child. What are the most important things you want the people working with your child to know? What are their interests? What makes them happy? What makes them miserable? What are the accommodations on the Individualized Education Program? (Yes, the people who work with your child should have a copy of

the IEP, or at least the relevant information on the IEP.) The beginning of a term can be busy and stressful, so providing this "one page" might be really helpful, and therefore gratefully received. Plus you'll feel reassured that you've done your due diligence.

- Begin the term with optimism and positivity. In fact, say it to yourself: "This is going to be a great year, and if something comes up that concerns me, I trust that I can work it out with my parents, teachers, school, or district." (Refer to "Set Team Agreements," page 9.) If you happen to have a team meeting scheduled for early in the term, it is a good idea to establish a communication plan among team members. And don't forget to apply this to your communication with team members *between* meetings.

- Even if it's not the beginning of the school year, use any excuse to start fresh. Much like changing our clocks in spring, there's no good reason we can't move forward on, say, Thanksgiving, Martin Luther King Day, Groundhog Day, or anytime that resetting to a new 'tude is needed. Make that pact with yourself and your team.

- Don't sweat the small stuff: keep things in perspective.

Anger Check

When I worked as a state mediator for the California Special Education Hearing Office, I saw there were more than 2,300 filings in one year alone! These are cases in which parents sued their school district over disagreements with their child's Individualized Education Program (IEP). The California Department of Education sent these parents a survey, asking what caused them to file for due process. The number-one reason wasn't about failing to get specific outcomes, such as a new placement or more services.

No; the main complaint was: *These people didn't feel heard.*

Think about it: When you get mad, is it always because you don't gain something specific, or is it often because you don't feel like your idea, complaint, or request is respectfully considered, understood, or valued? Examining my own experiences and observations within the world of school-parent relations and pondering the results of that survey, it dawned on me that saying, "I'm not feeling heard," is another way of saying, "My concerns are not being taken seriously enough for me to believe you care enough to help. And that makes me angry."

In a meeting or conversation when someone else is speaking, whether it's school-related or anywhere else, responses may arise that are – to put it politely – challenging. Maybe the feelings are even hotter because they're still smoldering from a prior encounter with the same speaker. Well, challenges don't necessarily defeat us. Sometimes we're able to overcome them, and that's a skill worth developing.

Take the example of a confrontational parent-teacher conference or – to add a layer of complication – let's say it is an IEP meeting in which the school psychologist is taking a parent through an official assessment of an autistic son. The more the psychologist talks, the more the parent is thinking, "This person clearly doesn't know my boy!" The blood is boiling. The jaw is clenched, and maybe so is a fist.

ADR provides a safe environment for revealing feelings.

When such high emotions come up in a meeting like this – especially if it seems on the edge of erupting into dangerous words or actions – don't just take a breath; take a break!

Anger is a common reaction to perceived unfairness, injustice, fear, embarrassment, or insults. Of all human emotions, anger is the hardest to manage. With that in mind, consider your reaction to such words as *yelling, fear, running,* and *fighting*. What are the first things that come to mind? For me, the best answer to that is "opportunity."

I believe that as long as we set team agreements (page 9), we should allow individuals to express their emotions, including anger. A fundamental concept of Alternative Dispute Resolution (ADR) is to provide a safe environment for revealing feelings – from which we can then move on, toward a collaborative outcome.

Let's be understanding and gentle. After all, this may (for example) be the first time parents hear that their child is probably not going to graduate with a high school diploma. They are allowed to have an emotional response, including the right to be angry. So is a special education teacher who wants to set up inclusion opportunities for her students, but is told by her general education teacher colleague that "those" students would disrupt learning for the "regular" students. Ouch!

We react to anger in several ways: we get angry ourselves, try to defuse the anger, or run away. As with fear, the most common individual reaction to anger is the proverbial fight-or-flight response. In ADR, we look for something of a compromise among these choices.

In almost every mediation that I have conducted, one party is angry or otherwise upset about something. We need to be prepared for this and also prepared to turn conflict into an opportunity whenever possible. We should enable the parties to collect themselves, and think more calmly about the situation.

Anger can often be defused by one simple technique: reassuring people that they are being heard! Not too long ago, I received a call from a parent who immediately said to me in an angry tone, "No one is listening to me!" I replied in a gentle voice, "I am listening to you now." I went on to say it was my hope that, after she was done telling me her story, she and I could come up with a plan for next steps and how she might get some resolution.

Her issue was how to obtain special-needs accommodations for her child, but her surface anger was the feeling of not being heard. By de-escalating that, she was able to recognize the underlying source of her anger, become less confrontational, and otherwise reasonably discuss and collaborate on finding a fair resolution for her child.

When faced with loud and angry voices in the middle of a mediation, it's easy to forget the basics. So here's the thing: rarely are people given permission to be angry. And that permission can be granted by any of us in the conflict resolution realm (which includes *you,* whatever role you have in it, or you wouldn't be reading this book!). In order to get past the anger and reach a place where they feel they are being heard, the listener (perhaps you) can employ skills and techniques to creatively help that angry person move forward, and thus turn a challenge into an opportunity.

Practicing This Skill

- Restate what the person says they are angry about, as reassurance you are listening. Often when a person feels heard, the anger lessens.
- Ask carefully worded questions. This can cause an angry person to slow down and think about the situation. (See "The Art of the Question," page 5.)
- Validate their right to be angry. Recognizing their source of anger and acknowledging those feelings may help them feel

less confrontational. (Slow, deep breathing is a good thing too. And a glass of water.)

- Speak quietly and slowly.
- If the other person is using inappropriate communication, hold your hand up in the "stop" position.
- In a crisis: stand up.
- Buy time to collect your thoughts: count and breathe.
- Take responsibility for your own anger and acknowledge your feelings. However, know that blaming decreases your personal power.
- Practice using "I" Messages (page 13).

The Role of Apology

When I got my driver's license at age seventeen, I remember my dad saying to me, "If you get into an accident, never admit fault." I reacted by saying something like, "But Dad, what about in a situation that I knew I was in the wrong? Or what if it was really an *accident* – like I didn't mean to cause any harm, but it happened because I was being careless?" His response: "Nope, don't say anything."

I realize that some other dads and most attorneys may disagree, but I believe there is a role for apology, and in many circumstances it can do wonders. As Lyn Johnson said, "An apology is the superglue of life. It can repair just about anything." If done right, an apology can help to mend relationships and can reestablish trust and respect.

We can probably relate to the two following examples.

An occupational therapist agrees he will meet with a child for thirty minutes each week, but a month passes without any such meeting. The parents learn this from the student, not from the therapist, and they are understandably upset. Did the specialist ignore their child, or maybe prioritize his time in favor of a different student? The parents are outraged and file a formal complaint.

Compare that to this example of a speech therapist who had to miss two weeks of work and there wasn't anyone to cover her caseload. On her return to work, she immediately contacted each of her clients' parents to personally apologize. It went something like this: "I am sorry for missing some sessions with Chris. I have calculated that I missed two thirty-minute sessions. So the way I can make this up is either to pull Chris out of class additional times, or I can make up the sessions after school. Whatever you prefer is fine with me." Her actions are prompt, she makes no excuses, and she offers concrete remedies. And the student is served!

> If done right, an apology can help to mend relationships and can reestablish trust and respect.

In the first scenario, it's too bad the occupational therapist didn't step up, the earlier the better, of course, and confess to misreading the agreement, or wrongly allowing a personal problem, like an impending divorce, to distract from professional attention. Whatever the context – by honestly owning the mistake, expressing remorse, and taking responsibility – he might have found the parents to be forgiving and sympathetic. Not only would everyone be spared from litigation but the relationship between the family and the therapist could even be strengthened by the expression of humanity and good intentions. And the student is served!

Certainly an apology is also warranted for those more spontaneous fouls, such as when a teacher, parent, specialist, or anyone else yells, makes personal attacks, and so on. Most people, even those targeted by such outbursts, respond positively to a genuine apology.

By "genuine" we mean clear and sincere. It's an apology that essentially states, "This is what I did wrong, I'm sorry for it, and here's how I will fix it." That tone can effectively diminish anger, as it humanizes the wrongdoer, who will now seem much less offensive or threatening. The overall effect on the relationship between family and school is to reinforce a feeling of positive "safety culture."

Even the one who needed to apologize can come away from the experience feeling good, with less self-reproach and more openness going forward. Those feelings will usually trump the comparatively feeble reasons for *avoiding* an apology: pride, reputation, fear of reprisal, and the like.

On the other hand, a bad apology only makes matters worse. You know – it's the half-hearted one that often starts with, "I'm sorry you feel this way, but…" It lacks empathy, is self-serving, and is frankly insulting. As Benjamin Franklin once put it, "Never ruin an apology with an excuse." A good apology is a nearly foolproof way to reduce tensions and otherwise enhance trust and teamwork.

Practicing This Skill

Think about a person that you might owe an apology. Write down what you did or didn't do that was a mistake. Then write down what you are going to do to correct the mistake. Get feedback from a trusted friend or colleague. Then, if you feel comfortable, go ahead and give it a try.

Early Conflict Resolution...
for the Grown-ups!

*T*his is about early intervention, a term we use a lot for our students, but before you roll your eyes and say, "I've heard that before," please keep reading. There are a couple of twists here. The emphasis on early intervention is vital enough to bear repeating. For that matter, periodically revisiting any important idea is a worthwhile "skill" that I embrace, as evidenced by several themes intentionally recurring throughout this book!

Anyway, let's get to the first of two points. While early intervention programs and strategies have been solidly in place for our students, what about our adults? What systems are installed at our school sites so that professionals and parents work better together? Surely we agree that when grown-ups express consistent messages and "speak the same language," then something wonderful happens for the students. Ideas, techniques, and behaviors are being modeled for them. And as teaching methods go, there's nothing more powerful and enduring than that, right?

When challenging conversations come up – and they always do – our best chance for successful resolution occurs when professionals and parents are already prepared to handle them with minimal confusion and conflict. Such disturbances and complications can inflict collateral damage on students. I highly recommend that each school takes time at the beginning of the school year to engage staff – *and parents, whenever possible* – in order to establish norms for practicing positive communication techniques, collaboration, and consensus.

You know what? Those exact qualities and goals are part of the graduation proficiency standards mandated by the state (see "Modeling the Common Core," page 38). As they say, "It's not just a good thing to do; it's the law!"

Which brings me to the second point. The focus of my practice is to work with teams at school sites to meet that key compliance standard by slightly adapting what I have always done: fostering effective communication and positive partnerships. What will vary slightly is greater emphasis on training the trainers so that instructors, staff members *(and don't forget parents)* can adapt the materials and teach these skills to their students.

> There's never a bad time to establish agreements and norms.

The start of the school year, when we're hopefully rested and there hasn't been time for conflict, is a good opportunity for establishing agreements on how we should all interact, especially when the need arises to have a challenging conversation. An example is a situation where two fourth-grade teachers are having a conflict. Luckily, prior to the first day of school, the staff went through a process in which they set norms and agreements on how they are going to communicate and support each other.

One of the teachers in question approached a colleague to discuss the issue (and gossip a little), and that person was able to redirect her to the agreements that were already in place – one of which was that they would always communicate to the source and not get people involved who didn't have anything to do with the conflict. As a result, the two feuding teachers found a good place and time to talk about their conflict without involving everyone else. In the previous year – before any such communication ground rules were in place – the whole school would have found out about it; the campus community would be uncomfortable; and general morale would suffer.

To be clear, even though the beginning of the year is a good starting point, there's never a bad time to establish agreements and norms. When

I'm working with people who are in conflict, I will use any excuse to help them move forward. Working with someone in February, I might say "In the spirit of Valentine's Day," or in January, "In the spirit of Martin Luther King's birthday" – any incentive to give people a fresh start.

Practicing This Skill

- With your team: imagine that it is the annual review of your group effort (an Individualized Education Program team, for example) and the first thing you must do is evaluate your present levels. Answer the following questions:
  - How are you all doing as a team? What's working? How are you communicating? How are you supporting one another? What areas might need some support?
  - Once you've completed the present levels, imagine that you are all meeting a year later. "Now" what does supporting one another look like? What does your communication plan look like? What has improved based on last year's evaluation?
  - What is it you want to be doing? How do you want to be communicating? How do you want to be working together? What do you need from teammates in order to achieve your goals? Your plan is a working document and there is always an opportunity to update and make improvements – meaning you don't have to wait a year to have your IEP review meeting.
  - Note: If things are presently going great, awesome! There's no need to *create* conflict. Congratulate each other with hearty high fives.
- Get your teammates to agree on using the formula in "Are You Ready for a Challenging Conversation?" (page 77).

Saying a Lot
Without Saying a Thing

Nonverbal communication is a powerful component of most conversations and it is certainly vital to active listening. When understood well – and performed well – it can be the key to having a positive meeting. However, poor nonverbal communication can blow up everything, resulting in low productivity, mistrust and, for those of you in special education, possibly even a due-process filing.

Have you ever been in a meeting where someone is silently but obviously shaking their head in disgust? What about the people texting or checking email during a presentation of results from an important report? These are examples of negative nonverbal communication. The same is true for slouching, making faces, crossing arms, and looks of confusion or disapproval. In virtual meetings, if someone's camera is off, it may be perceived similarly to texting, or feel as if that person's back is turned to members of the team.

For all such cases, these expressions may be inaudible – and even unintentional – but, as the saying goes, "Actions speak louder than words," and they sure can be annoying and discouraging, if not damaging. Note that typically the main takeaway from a meeting is not what was said but what was felt, and the reason cited most often for complaints and litigation is a feeling of not having been heard.

So, first be self-aware, as in being sure you're not the one who is seen as acting badly. Be attentive to reactions you elicit from others, and avoid off-putting mannerisms and behaviors that may not be intentional but nonetheless make a poor impression, such as the all-too-common offense of hiding behind your computer.

Meanwhile, always strive to recognize and emphasize *positive* nonverbal communication that allows all parties to know they *are* being heard, appreciated, and encouraged. Examples can include head nods, earnest note-taking, eye contact, and alert posture.

> The reason cited most often for complaints and litigation is a feeling of not having been heard.

Have you ever been at Individualized Education Program (IEP) team meetings with participants (notably parents) who share something undoubtedly difficult for them to talk about, perhaps something that makes them emotional? What nonverbal communication did you use to let them know you were listening? It could be as simple as leaning forward in your chair to show your interest, along with eye contact and a warm smile to show your empathy.

To employ these techniques, you don't have to be like a trained actor, pretending to feel something. Nor do you need to be like a poker master, able to spot another player's "tell." Just do your best to be observant, sincere, and maintain good intentions. (And why on earth are you doing this if you don't value those qualities?)

After all, it is important to be conscious of both the signals you send, as in conveying as much support and inclusion as possible, as well as those you receive. In the latter case – when you may be on the wrong end of troubling nonverbal communication – you can call on techniques to safely defuse or reverse the situation before the meeting is undermined.

That starts by establishing an environment of trust, where positive communication skills are rewarded, and it's okay to voice a question or concern. When facilitating meetings, one of my first objectives is to collaborate on setting some procedural norms and expectations (see "Set Team Agreements," page 9). That includes asking participants if they have any practical or process needs to disclose. For example, in a virtual meeting, someone might say, "So sorry, but I can't have my camera on because I'm driving," or the site administrator at an in-person meeting might say, "I'm on call today, so if there's an emergency on the other side of campus, I may have to excuse myself for a bit."

By alerting everyone to such needs at the beginning of the meeting, the team will be more understanding and supportive. That's much more acceptable and helpful than the displeasure and disrespect felt if, all of a sudden, a camera is off or someone just gets up and leaves the room.

During a meeting, if something comes up that is conspicuously distracting or just doesn't feel right or safe, one can gently and professionally, including appropriate body language, call it out by asking a nonthreatening question.

Examples:

- "Chris, I notice you are texting. Do you need to take a break?"
- "Alex, you haven't said much today, but by your head-shaking, it seems we may not be in agreement. Why don't we pause and check in on your concerns?"
- "Terry, I can tell by that quizzical look that there may be some confusion. May I clarify something for you?"
- "Dr. Jones, do you know your nose is bleeding?"

Bottom line: Have the confidence and techniques in hand to check in with that person. (Also review the chapters on "The Art of the Question," page 5, and "The Elephant in the Room," page 43.)

A related note: Listen with your eyes too! Good communication requires active listening, which is more than hearing words. If a speaker gets a response like, "That's exactly what I mean," it may *say* agreement, but what if it's *meant* as sarcasm? Note the *tone* of voice as well as other physical expressions, like gasps and sighs. And don't ignore quiet participants who ought to be brought into the conversation.

Practicing This Skill

- Find a trusted colleague or friend and ask for feedback regarding your nonverbal communication style. Start with the positives, and ask to hear what works. Does your body language match your words?

- If you're really gutsy, watch yourself in a recorded situation and assess what you did, again starting with the positives. (We should always remember to be gentle with ourselves.)
- To sharpen observation skills and inclusion techniques, take turns role-playing the scenario below with a handful of colleagues at work or friends at home. (Warning: This exercise may be great fun.)
  1. Choose a Speaker to talk for two to three minutes on any subject.
  2. Three or four Listeners will each draw from a hat a written "attitude" (bored, enthusiastic, angry, suspicious, impressed, distracted, confused, etc.) that they will express – without words – in response to the speech.
  3. If and when each attitude is identified by the Speaker, the Speaker will gently and professionally call out that Listener.
- A wrap-up discussion can review how the exercise illustrated the pitfalls of sending and receiving nonverbal communication, as well as assessing how to deal with it so it doesn't become an elephant in the room (see page 43).

The Power of
Showing Appreciation

A director of special ed called me the other day, wanting my help with a case, and I said, "I need you to call me when something positive is happening." This was a joke because, let's face it, when your job is mostly about mediating disputes involving school programs, you're not getting many calls from school districts or parents when they are happy with what's going on. Families, teachers, administrators, district personnel – **nearly everybody within a complex, busy school community – has very little time to slow down and show appreciation.**

No matter what our role may be, the work is hard. No matter what time of year it is, there is always a lot going on. For the moment, let's focus on the school part of the team. Servicing your students, conducting assessments, writing reports, attending to district, state, and federal requirements, and of course communicating with colleagues and parents on a daily basis: these are all on your plate (and I'm sure I missed other high-caliber bullet points on your list of responsibilities).

Throughout all this effort in fulfillment of your duties, who's telling you, "I saw you working with this student, and I was so impressed, seeing how you were able to keep his attention," or "Thank you for your report; it was great how specific you were with suggestions on how best to work with this student." Kind words of support are not as abundant as they should be, which is why I believe **teams should consciously set time aside to show appreciation for each other.**

Expressing it doesn't have to be about the Big Issue itself, whatever that may be. It can be offered in praise of a person's intelligence, generosity, creativity, emotional literacy, kindness, integrity, work ethic, practical skills, dignity, leadership ability, honesty, playfulness, practical wisdom, tact – or any other positive attribute the person possesses.

I know that expressing appreciation can be hard, and it can even be harder to be on the receiving end. I am not a psychologist, so I don't fully understand why, but I find in the work I do that individuals tend to have a harder time being open to taking in positive information and kind words than they do accepting negative feedback such as criticism, reprimands, or even condemnations. I want to give credit to Claude Steiner, who introduced me to the "positive-stroke economy." He works with individuals and organizations in Northern California, creating a positive-stroke culture.

It's vital that we develop a culture that puts **focus on what's working well rather than what we are doing wrong.** This really connects with the advantages of building a "Yes, and..." team (see page 69). If we are on the "Yes, but..." team, it's going to be a lot more depleting than a "Yes. and..." environment. When I look at certain campuses and their retention of staff, it is clear that schools built on voicing gratitude and recognizing excellence have less turnover – and more overall stability – than those focused largely on the negatives, or that never made this concept a priority.

I also see a correlation with parent relationships in terms of trust and satisfaction with their child's school experience. It's a comparatively simple and easy way – yet a high-impact way – to provide **something we all need, namely support for each other.** Let's face it: if we don't give specific validations to each other, nobody else will.

Now let's bring this idea into the Individualized Education Program (IEP) team meeting. I always suggest that parents begin the meeting with at least one sincere appreciation for someone on the team. If we start with that moment of positivity, it sets a tone for the rest of the meeting. If you are reading this as a parent, perhaps as part of a support group, family center, or a community advisory council (CAC), I encourage you to make sure that you're in a culture of "Yes, and…" and showing appreciation for each other.

Just like the school examples above, I have been to many CAC meetings where the norm is to focus on complaining about the school district rather than saying anything positive or providing any useful tools, thereby alienating many parents and community members who are there looking simply for some support.

Practicing This Skill

- Before stating an appreciation, ask permission: "Chris, may I give you a compliment?"
- Set time at the beginning of a staff or parent meeting for recognizing successes, offering special thank-yous, sharing good news, and so on.
- Ask a general question like, "What did anyone notice that a colleague did in the past month that made a situation better?" It can be a way to spark multiple expressions of appreciation.
- Each appreciation should be specific and simple: "Dr. Wilson, when you took time to sit with me yesterday and discuss the concerns I have about my daughter, it showed me you really care," or, "Thank you for making me laugh; you bring balance into my day."
- When receiving an appreciation, breathe in; take it in; appreciate it. Resist the inclination to return the praise right back to the person who just acknowledged you. It cheapens the moment.
- Note that expressions of appreciation are more beneficial when offered to a specific person rather than a group.

Look for Smaller Agreements and Celebrate Them

We often come to a meeting with an ambitious agenda. We want it to be productive, meaningful, and completed within a reasonable amount of time because we know that the professionals and parents that we work with are committed but also very busy and typically wear many hats. So, ready or not, we charge straight for the full outcome. It's "Big Agreement or Bust!" We pass for the end zone from eighty yards away. We try to eat the holiday turkey in one gulp. Results: incompletion and indigestion.

There is great satisfaction – and likelier goal-reaching – by managing a ball-control drive and taking tasty, bite-size portions. It's the same for seeking, recognizing, and capitalizing on smaller agreements. It works for just about any meeting, but for practical purposes, let's focus here on the Individualized Education Program (IEP) team meeting.

Talk about ambitious: the federal government mandated a comprehensive agenda for IEP teams to follow. Plus, as we all know, the decision-making process is to be done by consensus. To have the best shot at accomplishing all this, small agreements should be spotted and pointed out.

For instance, at the outset of a meeting, you can ask, "Is everyone here ready to talk about Taylor?" When they nod, you have your first agreement. Honor it! Just getting a full team together is an achievement that at least calls for quiet applause. If the team reaches consensus that math is Taylor's strength, that's another one. Honor it! A roomful of "thumbs up" perhaps? If everyone concurs that Taylor's time on task needs to improve? Yep: another agreement and worthy of a gentle fist-bump. Heck, after a few more meetings like that, there could be a rowdy round of high fives!

> **Even the process of pulling out calendars for ten minutes to find a next date and time that works may be called an agreement.**

But don't expect that right away. Sometimes emotions flare up in these meetings (a passionate parent, perhaps) but don't allow it to confound the work. Instead, seek recognition from the entire team that the parent clearly cares deeply and wants the best for Taylor – just as they all do. *Ding-ding:* agreement! For that matter, when seemingly little is accomplished and rescheduling is required, even the process of pulling out calendars for ten minutes to find a next date and time that works may be called an agreement. Honor that too by expressing how you look forward to seeing everyone then.

As a tougher example, let's say Taylor currently receives weekly occupational therapy, but a complete assessment by the occupational therapist (OT) concludes that this should be discontinued. At the IEP team meeting, the district members agree with the OT. But the parents cry foul, despite bringing no objective information to support their position – unlike the OT, who has read the "Use Objective (Legitimate) Criteria" chapter (page 25), including offering a prior meeting with the parents to address their questions (hint, hint).

In any case, don't give up! You are not yet ready to say, "Let's call the mediator," or "File for due process!" or "I am going to get an attorney and we will see about this." Below are examples of possible small agreements that can be used in this situation:

- Question strategies, as discussed in "The Art of the Question" (page 5), help the district part of the team discover the interests of the parents, knowing how important it is to be "Separating Interests from Positions" (page 22).

- The chair, OT, and parents meet informally to further air concerns.
- The team authorizes another OT assessment by someone new, with a follow-up IEP team meeting scheduled to discuss that assessment and recommendations.

Note that I avoided jumping to Big Agreement conclusions. Taylor's case figures to require long-term or compromise solutions. First things first – like honoring small agreements.

Practicing This Skill

- At the end of each meeting, allow time for the team to make some lists. First, facilitate a discussion on the smaller agreements of that day and then make a list of the disagreements. It would have been easy (but unsatisfying) in the example above to focus only on the OT disagreement without any acknowledgment of the agreements, no matter how small.
- Focus on the positives. Remember, parent and school teams are relationships, and relationships flourish when we emphasize the good things. If you find this hard to do, revisit "The Power of Showing Appreciation" (page 63) and practice some of the tips there.
- I started this chapter with a sports analogy which – if you know me – is pretty impressive, as I don't know much about sports. However, I am a huge fan of huddles because that's where they might be saying, "Have a great game!" or "Go get 'em!" or "We got this!" That gave me the idea to recommend that school-parent teams might start off a meeting with a huddle – one that agrees to keep up the hard work, knowing it takes a team to succeed, and we ought to celebrate that!

"Yes, and..." or "Yes, but..."

Improvisational actors are amazing, and great improv scenes, not just the funny ones, are always memorable and effective. Performing well without a script requires openness, imagination, discipline, keen responses, and training. But everyday life is not scripted either. That makes us all improvisers, performing the best we can in our daily tasks, interactions, meetings, and the like. So we too can benefit from training and sharpening our skills. That's where this book comes in, especially this chapter, which is directly inspired by the core improv technique called "Yes, and..."

To illustrate: The scene opens at Parent Night, when a mom walks up to a teacher and says, "You're giving my child too much homework!" The teacher replies, "Yes, but it's not too much homework for my other students." Now suppose that scene instead starts with the teacher walking up to the parent and saying, "Do you know that your child never completes the daily homework?" to which the mom replies, "Yes, but your assignments are uninteresting and just seem like an excessive heap of busywork."

In both scenarios, the stage has been set for a conflict bound to reach an unhappy ending. Why? Because both replies began with "Yes, *but...*" when they could've started with "Yes, *and...*" as in, "Yes, and I can see how a lot of homework may be overwhelming in some circumstances. Does your child have a regular time and place to study?" Likewise from the parent: "Yes, and of course homework is important, so I wonder if there might be ways to streamline the assignments, or maybe rotate in some lighter workload days?"

These "Yes, and..." responses are better because they are more respectful and leave openings for further conversation, cooperation, and compromise. Both parties are good listeners who acknowledge, appreciate, and accept each other's perspective, ideally setting aside egos and agendas. Theirs is a high-potential partnership, mutually committed to a greater goal, namely advancing a child's education.

> Yes, and..." responses are more respectful and leave openings for further conversation, cooperation, and compromise.

It's like a character in an improv introducing a second character by addressing him as "your royal highness," but the second actor had a predetermined intention to enter the scene as, say, a clumsy waiter. He wasn't ready to acknowledge the "reality" established by his scene partner. He wasn't open to – not prepared for – adapting his mind-set from clumsy waiter to royal highness. If only the second actor willingly accepted the circumstances set by the first actor, he might have had fun treating the other character with royal arrogance, or behaving like a royally clumsy king. Instead, the scene was botched, all because he broke the first rule of improv: Always commit to "Yes, and..."

This brings to mind a related chapter in this book, "Don't Argue Mentally" (page 28), as it speaks to the mistake of having preconceptions about a given situation, of fixing upon your own views at the cost of hearing others.

Saying "Yes, but..." shuts down the collaborative nature of what a school-parent relationship should look like. This is true for all teams and relationships. "Yes, and..." leads to progress, and let's be clear: "Yes, and..." does not necessarily mean "I agree." For example, at an Individualized Education Program (IEP) meeting, parents ask for a one-to-one aide for their child. The immediate response by the district representative might be, "Yes, but there are already three adults in the classroom." From this, the parents could easily get defensive and shut down the collaboration.

The district representative could have responded with, "Yes, and tell me more," or, "Yes, and what would that look like?" or, "Yes, and what's happening now that causes you to bring this request?" Those open questions lead to a more thoughtful conversation. In fact, "The Art of the Question" (page 5) and "Separating Interests from Positions" (page 22) are also must-reads to gain added insight and skill at handling these situations.

The truth is, I get a lot of pushback on the "Yes, and..." concept, because the fear is that we are conveying more agreement than we intend. My long experience has shown otherwise, as it has proved to be an effective tool for many successful teams. If you're nervous about saying "Yes, and..." remember that it is essentially jargon – a very useful kind of jargon we want to be using in our teams. So it's fine for you to substitute "Yes, and..." with other phrases that also reflect active listening and openness. For instance: "I appreciate what you said because..."

Practicing This Skill

We have the ability to step back and decide what kind of team we want to be. The exercises below are a way to practice the skill as a team. When you get together to formulate ground rules about how you'll work together and support each other, take a survey of the participants about whether you're a "Yes, and..." team or a "Yes, but..." team. If you agree that you want to be a "Yes, and..." team, come up with specific examples of what that would look like – and write them into your team agreements (page 9).

- Role-play in three parts:
  1. "Yes, but..."

     Pick someone (maybe whoever has the shortest hair) to take on the role of the one planning a vacation for all group members. The others play the part of friends or colleagues who tend to "always spot the problem." They will begin each sentence by saying "Yes but..." For this exercise, try not to ask questions.

2. "Yes, and..."

    Whoever has the longest hair in the group will plan the vacation for the group. This time your friends or colleagues show appreciation and may even add suggestions. They will begin each sentence by saying "Yes, and..." For this exercise, try not to ask questions.

3. Once the group has had about five minutes per scenario to play out this exercise, it's time to debrief. Start with the group that resisted and contradicted the speaker (the "Yes, but..." group); then turn to the ones who employed the active listening skills that allowed the planner to feel heard and validated (the "Yes, and..." group). Compare what happened and how it felt in each. After that, open up the discussion to share people's experiences in situations where each approach dominated.

- "Yes, and..." works in personal relationships too. Do try this at home!

Spot the Bullying; Stop the Bullying

A parent support group recently asked me to facilitate a workshop titled "Bullying: What Is It? Working Together to Figure This Out." I tried to get out of it, suggesting that I had no expertise in this area, that a school psychologist or counselor would be better qualified. But they insisted I was "the man for the job," so I went about putting together a program.

The real story is that I didn't want to do a workshop on bullying because it hit too close to home. Childhood memories of being bullied never go away; they just get pushed below the surface. Now here they were, coming for me again. I couldn't help but wonder why I was chosen to lead this workshop. Must I suffer old wounds? Might it provide me with some free therapy?

Then I thought, "Hold on; it's not about me." I refocused on this job I have enjoyed for so many years, and about how lucky I am to be able to bring parents, school district personnel, and outside professionals together, all doing their best to advocate for their children or students.

Something else dawned on me. The bully might be spotted nearer than we thought – it might be a team member; it might even be you! After all, when we get caught up in advocating for a cause that has special importance to us, all our previously learned mediation skills and positive communication habits may go out the window. The stakes become so high that advocacy turns to competition. We so much want to *win* that, although we are adults, we take on bullying characteristics. If that is ever the case with you – and I'm telling you from personal experience as someone who had an Individualized Education Program (IEP) growing up – please stop it!

> We so much want to *win* that, although we are adults, we take on bullying characteristics.

We students are watching you. We learn from you. You are our role models. We want and need you to advocate for us, but despite our disabilities, we are smart enough and intuitively know when you go overboard. We know when it becomes less about us and more about the fight: your fight. We may then pick up behaviors that you are modeling or – just as bad – we may get embarrassed or anxious about them, then cover up that pain by repressing our feelings and behavior. After all, we are children with disabilities, and we don't want to get you mad out of fear you will stop advocating for us.

So, in those cases when you feel that no one is listening or that your hard work is not being recognized, please remain an adult. Be aware of rising tensions, especially your own, because that can escalate the intensity – even desperation – of our communication styles, including turning to the characteristics of bullying. (Some may call it harassment.)

We all know the topic of bullying has gained recent media attention, and that has prompted such positive measures as schools and districts developing curricula, task forces, and sharper disciplinary policies. So why am I writing about this here? It's because students with disabilities are among the most likely targets of bullying, and also less able to stand up for themselves. They rely on you – parents, teachers, specialists, and administrators – to keep them safe and healthy. The last thing they need is to put that trust in you only to observe you yelling, using foul language, and otherwise putting each other down, supposedly on their behalf!

We know that our students are going to experience our behavior, and model their own behavior from it. Obviously then, it's far better for them to see us settling disagreements by sitting down to talk, listen, and brainstorm in reasonable ways.

So how do we spot that bully in the IEP meeting? Well, first, we have to go back to the principles in the "Set Team Agreements" chapter (page 9). That's about the vital necessity of establishing meeting agreements – ground rules – for conducting our team meetings, as well as our interactions with team members between meetings. I can't overstate the importance of having the baseline of team agreements. Without them, we have no agreed-on fallback position or do-over if somebody in the meeting starts up a rant, such as bullying others in the room.

Dealing with a situation like that is much easier if the solution might be as straightforward as invoking the ground rules that *all* participants had agreed on earlier. If that agreement was never established, or is being ignored in this moment, try other measures, depending on the circumstances and how you feel, such as, in no particular order:

- End the meeting. No one gets paid enough to be abused.
- Take a de-escalation break that might serve as an opportunity to call someone in rather than call them out. The last thing we want to do is become the bully, so discreetly take that person aside and maybe ask, "What's going on for you when this behavior is happening?"
- When in doubt, have empathy. A thing that helps me work with challenging people is to imagine what it's like to be in their shoes. I will create a story (it may even be true) about all the terrible things this person had to go through, either as a child or even last night. Don't get me wrong; I know that doing this can be tough. Almost as tough as:
- Don't take things personally. Examples: "This is my child we are talking about!" and, "This is my job at stake here!" Just like every other skill in this book, practice helps. I can say, happily, that this is something that does get better with age and years of experience.

Practicing This Skill

- When in a challenging meeting with that challenging person, practice the strategies outlined above. After the meeting, debrief with someone you trust, maybe someone who was in this same meeting. Or consider talking about it during one of our virtual office hours sessions!

- Review the other chapters. The handier you are with the tools in your entire kit, the less likely you are to lapse into inappropriate behavior.
- Imagine you are the child or student you are advocating for, then ask yourself if you are making him or her proud, or if your emotions are getting the best of you.
- Check in with your child or student, or at least someone you trust to be honest and objective, to gauge whether you are maintaining your professional poise.

Are You Ready for a Challenging Conversation?

If you have a good grasp of the themes and techniques offered in this book, then you are ready to effectively handle challenging conversations like those described in each chapter. Maybe you are a longtime professional educator, such as a school principal, district administrator, counselor, teacher, or service provider. Maybe you are a young parent with little or no experience interacting with school personnel. Whatever your background, your role in the conversation is equally important, and it's best to be prepared – for the sake of the child or student you are *all* there to serve.

The conversation might be an Individualized Educational Program (IEP) team meeting involving a handful of people. It might be an appointment with the principal or a one-on-one parent-teacher conference. It might be a program or policy discussion that's part of a crowded PTA meeting or a proposal presentation at a staff meeting. Regardless of the situation, the main challenge of a challenging conversation is to be up for the challenge!

Challenging is one of those all-purpose words that – in context here – might cover any or many other words, such as *difficult, controversial, serious, stressful, treacherous,* or *awkward.* It's also a word that makes some people nervous. So if it is a trigger for you, please replace it with another. Come to think of it, the step-by-step formula below may apply to *any* good and productive conversation. It was not created by me, and to be honest, I can't find where this originally came from. (Whoever you are, thank you!)

In any case, let's say you have thoughtfully worked through this book and you feel your sharpened skill set and perspectives are ready for action. So step right up now; there is an upcoming conversation you need to have...

Step-by-Step Guidelines for Handling a Challenging Conversation

Step 1. Commit to work it out.

- Find a good time and place to talk.
- Agree to *try your best* to solve the problem.
- Establish ground rules (see "Set Team Agreements," page 9).

    When selecting a place to talk, it's best to pick a neutral location: one that provides no advantage to anybody but still feels comfortable and pleasant. A local coffeehouse or park may do nicely. True, these may come with distractions, but they can provide a level of confidentiality that comes with being away from, say, a workplace, especially if the conversation or meeting is between colleagues who are dealing with a work conflict.

Step 2. Define the problem.

- Each person says what happened and how they feel.
- Use active listening (page 1) and "I" Messages (page 13).
- Focus on needs and interests (page 22).

    I find it helpful for each person to have paper and a pen, so that instead of interrupting a speaker, they may make notes to know their thoughts won't be forgotten when it is their turn to speak.

Step 3. Brainstorm solutions.

- Suggest many ways to address the issue.
- Do not judge the suggestions.

When brainstorming, it is necessary for everyone to feel comfortable tossing ideas around. So it's important not to judge the suggestions of other participants. If the participants are not feeling comfortable yet, then this brainstorming step may be premature, and more time is needed on Steps 1 and 2.

Step 4. Choose a solution and make an action plan.

- Consider all options; look at possible outcomes.
- Select a solution that *everyone* agrees to.
- Decide the specifics (Who? What? Where? When? How?)

The last point is extremely important and is sometimes overlooked. When we get to Step 4, we need to be as specific as possible. An example: The science department at a middle school agrees to treat everyone with respect. It's important to ask, What does this look like? How will we be communicating with each other? This same team also agrees to meet regularly throughout the year to make sure everyone is on the same page. It's important to determine: How often is the team going to meet? When will the meetings take place? What's the length of these meetings? What criteria will we use to define our success? And so on.

I recommend documenting all the agreements that were reached in the meeting, and have all the participants sign it. Each participant should have a copy of the agreement for their records. This document can be as formal or informal as the participants want, although my suggestion is always to make them as simple and easy to read as possible.

Practicing This Skill

Using the formula for having a challenging conversation takes practice, practice, practice – such as playing out a scenario. The first time, pick someone you trust, and keep the stakes low. Perhaps it's evaluating a past trip you've taken with this person, and then planning the next one. It really can be about anything. Feel free to use me as an excuse to practice this formula with a colleague or spouse. You might say, "I am reading this communication book, and the author is making us practice using this skill. Will you be willing to try this with me?"

When Things Go Wrong, Don't Despair, Repair!

When you have a bumpy meeting, it may feel like a minor fender-bender or a major crash. Either way, what do you do? You can ignore it and live with the damage, or you can repair it – and hopefully learn from it. In a school setting, such as an Individualized Education Program (IEP) team meeting, those repairs are necessary because the most injured party may be the student, whose well-being is the purpose of that meeting in the first place.

All participants in a school meeting (parents, staff, *everyone*) should remember that their common objective is a positive student outcome. By keeping focus on that fact, there is greater likelihood of cooperation instead of conflict; recognizing that **we are not on opposing "sides" but instead are all in this together** and will equally benefit by setting a tone of mutual good will. Besides, nobody wants to deal with the alternative of getting entangled in the impersonal formality and jeopardy of legalistic due process.

This doesn't mean every issue can be easily resolved. Collaboration takes effort, and we're all human. Accidents happen, as do mistakes and misunderstandings. Emotions and biases arise. Yet there's never a bad time to remind each other of our shared priority and commitment to work on behalf of students. In that spirit – when taking part in these discussions – we urge you to adopt our favorite phrase at Purchin Consulting: **"Let's be hard on the problem, and gentle with each other."**

Sometimes parents arrive at an IEP meeting already angry. Maybe they're expecting a negative response because requests to provide a personal aide for their child have been denied three times. Sometimes a school official arrives at an IEP meeting weary and distracted, having been in three other stressful IEP meetings earlier that day. These are legitimate reasons for their negative demeanor, but bear in mind that **behavior is communication, whether or not the message is intentional,** and negativity shuts out productivity. When a meeting starts badly, the odds say it will end badly too unless somebody, like you, steps in to limit the damage, if not reverse it.

If you promptly recognize that your meeting has gone off the road, you can probably steer it back on course. Go ahead and face the problem, but with openness, even kindness. You can sincerely address the aforementioned angry parents (and similarly, the distracted administrator) with something nonconfrontational like, "Before we get started, I sense that something may be on your mind. Please tell us about it so that we might clear the air and offer support."

> Knowing we have common objectives makes it easier to identify common ground.

Another hazard to avoid is having someone decide to surprise the group with a distracting or inflammatory issue. Example: A parent arrives at the meeting accompanied by an unexpected friend, ally, or advocate. By suddenly changing the cast of characters, the story changes, and the original characters (in this case, school officials) resent the new plot twist. Another example: A school psychologist surprises the parent by waiting until the meeting to disclose new information from an evaluation of the student. This too becomes a disruptive plot twist, leaving others (in this case, the parents) unprepared.

Those actions are allowed, but in each case, there could have been advance notice and discussion about adjusting the agenda. There is a lot of value in front-loading a meeting, such as a parent giving notice of bringing a friend to the IEP, or the school psychologist providing parents with a review of their findings prior to the meeting. If you're bringing entirely new personnel or information to the meeting, let the others prepare for it. What's the name and role of this new person who will be joining us? What does the new psych eval reveal?

By showing such consideration or professional courtesy, you will demonstrate the right spirit of collaboration and good intentions, and the effect is likely to advance a harmonious resolution instead of an angry roadblock. **Surprises tend to breed defensiveness or distrust,** and a lack of trust prevents healthy communication.

Studies reveal that our strongest takeaway from a meeting is how we felt about it, more so than what was said there. That's all the more reason to have your antenna up during these conversations, watch-

> Building the relationships within a team, and rebuilding them when necessary, is an ongoing process.

ing for revealing reactions that may be unspoken but are "loud and clear" in other ways, notably body language. This is why it's a good strategy to **"check in" periodically with participants.** Doing that may be as simple as asking gentle questions, such as, "Is anyone unclear about that last point?" and "Maybe some of you are uncomfortable with that idea. Shall we talk more about it?"

Perhaps some members of the IEP team have a pet complaint about, say, punctuality. For them, starting late is a sign of disrespect. So if you arrive late, they are angry from the start, and that anger morphs into time-wasting comments about wasting time! Solution: Be sure you're always early for those meetings. And yes, if *they* arrive after you (or are late themselves), don't make a big deal about *their* punctuality. Just go forward with the agenda. Your show of patience and mature prioritization could set a win-win tone for that meeting, as well as for future meetings with the same group.

Knowing we have common objectives makes it easier to identify common ground. And emphasizing common ground is a great way to overcome setbacks and obstacles. So do your best to tune in to your team members. What are some of their bad habits and triggers? Avoid them!

And what are their virtues and sources of pride? Boost them!

When a meeting gets contentious, try stepping back for a moment and changing the subject to prior points of agreement and progress. Is there a teacher that everyone knows to be caring and effective? Can we all recognize and applaud how diligently a particular set of parents organize their child's daily routine? Remember how grateful we were at how the principal handled that lunchtime incident last week?

Speaking of team members, don't just think of them during the IEP meeting itself. Remember that building the relationships within a team, and rebuilding them when necessary, is an ongoing process. It involves all the interactions between each team member, such as the communication between the parent and the teacher, or the teacher and the therapist. For good measure, beware of damage that can be done by *extended* team members. For example, how many parents decide they can't stand and won't trust the school principal? Why? Mainly because the office *receptionist* is rude!

Returning to the car crash metaphor: Might you have checked your mirrors and blind spots more frequently? And did you forget that pothole you hit the last time you took this road? Be on the lookout for problems that may be blossoming, and which you sure don't want to become full-flowered catastrophes. These are often foreshadowed when one of the team suddenly changes tone or behavior. Is this person becoming unresponsive to emails, or no longer coming to meetings well prepared?

These could be signs of unrelated personal problems, for which you could still gently offer support, such as allowing a lightened workload or temporary rescheduling. On the other hand, it could be that their "ghosting" you means an attorney is lurking behind the scenes.

Then there is the topic of apology. Acknowledging your missteps and saying you're sorry can be a huge plus, amply earning you credit and respect that far outweighs the momentary discomfort or embarrassment of your admission. And certainly it's better to apologize for a mistake than to double-down on it or cover it up. It's such a valuable topic that an entire chapter of this book elaborates on "The Role of Apology" (page 53).

More than anything, all team members must feel they are being heard.

Practicing This Skill

- Prevent problems by establishing periodic communication logs, and include established benchmarks and deadlines that everyone can see. It'll motivate everyone to stay on task and keep team members from claiming they weren't responsible because they weren't informed!
- The best we can all do is not give up. Things may go wrong. Maybe there are times we do get embroiled in state compliance complaints and other "due process" situations. Just remember that, as long as our children are in the school system, we can always come back to the issues, armed with more experience and ever-improving skills.
- This workbook (or at least the ideas in it) should not stay on the shelf or on the sidelines. Your team needs you; stay in the game!

Please Put Me Out of My Job

If I were to receive an email from you that said you've used skills in the book that made your teams more positive and successful, I would be a very happy camper.

If you said to me, "Marc, I have the best teams because, when we do have disagreements, we have a protocol (agreement) on how to work through our disagreements, and so we are eliminating the need to have an external mediator," I would be even more thrilled!

My hands are up high in support of every parent and school team being successful. May you have the spirit to want that too, and the confidence to do it, knowing you have the tools at your ready. When things get tough, feel free to check in. As long as I'm offering virtual office hours, stop by anytime. My website will have up-to-date information on how to find the meeting link – as long as I'm still working, that is.

I'm on your side because we're all on the same side: committed to do right by our children and students.

References and Web Links

Applied Improvisation Network (AIN):
www.appliedimprovisationnetwork.org

Center for Appropriate Dispute Resolution in Special Education
(CADRE): www.cadreworks.org

Purchin Consulting: www.purchinconsulting.com

Appendixes

1. Sample Prep Sheet Before Entering a Challenging Meeting

A printable version of the prep sheet appears on the next page. These concepts are from the *Getting to Yes* workbook by Roger Fisher and William Ury.

Prep Sheet Before Entering a Challenging Meeting

My Interests

List what matters to me: my wants and needs.

_____

_____

_____

Their Interests

List what I think they care about: their wants and concerns. Remember that each person in the meeting may have their own interests.

_____

_____

_____

Agreements

List the possible agreements we might reach.

_____

_____

_____

Objective Criteria

List the objective criteria that give my wants and needs legitimacy.

_____

_____

_____

My Walking-Away Alternatives

List what you can do if you walk away without an agreement. Consider what you would really do if you can't reach agreement and you are at an impasse.

_____

_____

_____

2. Suggested Template for an ADR Award
from the "Direct, Honest, Respectful" chapter, page 41

Alternative Dispute Resolution Skill Recognition Award

We can all learn from each other

Nominate a professional or a parent that has used positive Alternative Dispute Resolution skills (good communication techniques) to help resolve a conflict or potential conflict.

At a monthly meeting (staff meeting, school board meeting, community advisory meeting, and the like), a nominee will be chosen and the technique or skill that was used will be read out. The person whose technique is read will receive formal recognition from the district.

Information needed:

Name of person to be recognized: _____

District or school: _____

Briefly describe the situation and the tools that this person used:

_____

_____

_____

_____

_____

_____

Submissions are accepted year-round, and there is no limit to the number of submissions an individual can make. Self-nominations are also strongly encouraged.

About Purchin Consulting

Purchin Consulting's mission is to empower individuals and teams to have positive and productive working relationships, through training, coaching, meeting facilitation, and mediation.

About Marc Purchin

Marc Purchin's goals, education, experience, achievement, reputation, and vision combined to prompt the establishment of Purchin Consulting in 1997.

Marc has personally conducted more than three thousand mediations, mostly through contracts with the California Special Education Hearing Office, the Department of Developmental Disabilities, several public school districts, and numerous nonprofit organizations. In addition to that work, he has developed Alternative Dispute Resolution (ADR) programs for Special Education Local Plan Areas (SELPA) throughout the state of California.

Marc earned his bachelor's degree at Southern Illinois University, majoring in speech communication with an emphasis in interpersonal communication and theater. He then completed the distinctive master's in business administration (MBA) in nonprofit management offered by American Jewish University (formerly University of Judaism). That program added him to its faculty in 1996, and he has taught courses there such as "Conflict Resolution and Negotiation" and "Organizational Development and Leadership." Marc has also taught a "Collaboration" course in the School of Education at Cal State Dominguez Hills.